Granny's Favorites Cookbook

Granny's Favorites Cookbook

Dee Schoenmakers

Library of Congress Control Number: 2016905934
ISBN: Hardcover   978-1-5144-8414-2
                Softcover   978-1-5144-8413-5
                eBook   978-1-5144-8412-8

Print information available on the last page.

Rev. date: 05/02/2016

To order additional copies of this book, contact:
Xlibris
1-888-795-4274
www.Xlibris.com
Orders@Xlibris.com
736595

Contents

Breakfast Recipes

Lunch Recipes

Dinner Recipes

International Recipes

Salad Recipes

Side Dish Recipes

Party Recipes

Bread Recipes

Pasta Recipes

Dessert Recipes

Beverage Recipes

Condiment Recipes

Soup / Stew Recipes

♥ I dedicate this book to
seven generations of grannies
who contributed recipes to
Granny's Favorites Cookbook.
Many thanks. ♥

Have a wonderful time
preparing meals and treats
for your family!

Cooking Codes

Common Recipe Abbreviations

cup	c.
gallon	gal.
hour	hr.
minute	min.
ounce	oz.
pint	pt.
pound	lb.
quart	qt.
tablespoon (s)	tbsp.
teaspoon (s)	tsp.

For Good Measure

Salt, spices, baking powder, and baking soda. Fill the measuring spoon to overflowing, then level the spoon off using the blunt straight edge of a dull knife.

Flour or powdered sugar. Spoon the flour lightly into the measuring cup until overflowing. Use a knife to push excess flour off and level the cup. Do not pack the flour or shake the cup as you level it. If the recipe calls for sifted flour, sift the flour onto a square of waxed paper and then pour into the measuring cup.

Brown sugar. Spoon the brown sugar into the measuring cup, and pack it down tightly with the back of the spoon. Keep packing it until the sugar is level with the top of the cup.

Granulated sugar. Spoon the sugar into the measuring cup to overflowing and level with the edge of a knife. If sugar is lumpy, sift before measuring.

Milk, water, or other liquids. Set the liquid measuring cup on a level surface (such as a countertop), lower your head so you are at eye level with the cup, and slowly pour the liquid into the measuring cup until it reaches the desired level.

Shortening. Pack the shortening into the measuring cup and scrape off the excess. Briefly set the bottom of the measuring cup into hot water, and the shortening will slide right out.

If the recipe calls for_____, you will need the following

½ cup butter	1 stick or ¼ pound
2 Tbsp. butter	1 ounce
1 pound butter	4 sticks
1 square baking chocolate	1 ounce
2 ¼ cups brown sugar	1 pound
3 ½ cups powdered sugar	1 pound
2 cups granulated sugar	1 pound
4 cups white flour	1 pound
3 cups cooked rice	1 cup uncooked
2 cups cooked noodles	1 cup or 4 oz. uncooked
1 cup bread crumbs	2 slices of bread
1 cup cracker crumbs	12 graham crackers or 20 saltine crackers or 23 vanilla wafers
2 cups grated cheese	½ pound
1 cup chopped nuts	¼ pound
1 cup chopped celery	2 medium stalks
1 cup chopped onion	2 medium onions
1 cup chopped tomato	2 large tomatoes
1 cup diced green pepper	1 large pepper
1 cup chopped apples	1 medium apple
2 cups sliced strawberries	1 pint strawberries
3 tbsp. lemon juice	1 lemon
8 tbsp. orange juice	1 orange
1 tsp. grated lemon peel	1 lemon
2 tsp. grated orange peel	1 orange

1 cup egg yolks	14 eggs
1 cup egg whites	10 eggs
2 cups cooked hamburger	1 pound hamburger

Simple Substitutions

Simple ingredients can work double-time giving you great versatility and saving you a trip to the grocery store. The next time you cannot find buttermilk, cornstarch, or baking chocolate, look at this chart for a substitute.

If the recipe calls for_____, use this instead:

Dairy Products

½ cup butter	½ cup shortening plus ¼ tsp. salt
1 cup whipping cream	1/3 cup butter plus ¾ cup milk
½ cup buttermilk	½ cup milk plus 1 ½ tsp. vinegar
½ cup sour milk	½ cup milk plus 1 ½ tsp. lemon juice
1 cup whipped cream	1 egg white whipped with 1 sliced banana
1 cup whole milk	1 cup water, 4 tbsp. plus 2 tsp. melted butter or ½ cup water plus ½ cup evaporated milk
1 cup skim milk	1 cup water plus 4 tbsp. nonfat instant milk
½ cup honey butter	2 tbsp. butter plus ¼ cup honey
½ cup sour cream	½ cup plain yogurt
1 egg	2 egg yolks plus 1 tbsp. water or 1 tsp. unflavored gelatin mixed with tbsp. cold water and 2 tbsp. boiling water
2 egg whites	1 egg white plus 1 tbsp. ice water

Baking Ingredients

1 tsp. baking powder	½ tsp. cream of tartar
1 tbsp. flour to thicken	2 egg yolks or ½ tbsp. cornstarch or 2 tsp. quick-cooking tapioca
1 tsp. double-acting baking powder	1 ½ tsp. regular baking powder plus 1 ½ tsp. vinegar
1 cup cake flour	1 cup regular flour, minus 2 tbsp. + 2 tbsp. cornstarch
1 cup bread flour	½ cup flour plus ½ cup cornmeal, Bran, or whole wheat flour
1 package dry yeast	2 tsp. dry yeast or 1 cake compressed yeast
1 square unsweetened chocolate	3 tbsp. cocoa plus 1 tbsp. butter
½ cup molasses	1 cup honey
1 cup tomato juice	½ cup tomato sauce plus ½ cup water
1 cup wine	1 cup apple juice
1 cup beer	1 cup water
1 cup orange liqueur	1 cup orange juice
1 large marshmallow	10 miniature marshmallows
1 cup honey	1 ¼ cups sugar plus ¼ cup water
½ cup graham cracker crumbs	½ cup saltine cracker crumbs
1 can cream of celery soup	1 can cream of mushroom or 1 can cream of chicken soup

Seasonings

½ cup ketchup for cooking	½ cup tomato sauce, 1 tbsp. vinegar, and 1 cup sugar
1 tsp. dry mustard	1 tsp. prepared mustard
1 cup chopped onion	1/3 cup dehydrated onions
1 tsp. instant onion	4 tbsp. chopped fresh onion
1 tbsp. fresh parsley	1 tsp. parsley flakes

Fruits and Vegetables

Mandarin oranges	pineapple tidbits
8 oz. can grapefruit	1 medium fresh grapefruit
½ lb. fresh mushrooms	4 oz. can mushrooms
10 oz. frozen peas	8 oz. can peas
8 oz. whole tomatoes	8 oz. can stewed tomatoes

Miscellaneous

1 can chow mien	1 can potato shoestrings or 3 cups cooked rice
1 cup hominy	1 cup cooked rice
1 cup cooked rice	1 cup cooked noodles
1 cup seasoned bread crumbs	1 cup regular bread crumbs with 1 tsp. black pepper or 3 slices of cubed bread with 1 tsp. black pepper
½ cup pecans	½ cup walnuts or almonds
1 lb. ground pork	1 lb. ground beef
½ cup cubed ham	½ cup chopped luncheon meat
8 oz. can chili beans	8 oz. can kidney beans with 2 tsp. chili powder

Common Cooking Terms

Bake. To cook, either covered or uncovered, in an oven.

Baste. To keep foods moist during cooking by pouring or brushing liquid, such as meat drippings, melted fat, or another liquid, over them.

Beat. To make mixture cream smooth or filled with air by whipping in a brisk motion.

Blanch. To precook food briefly in boiling liquid, usually to loosen the skin. For example, drop tomatoes in boiling water for less than a minute and the skin comes off easily.

Blend. To stir two or more ingredients together until they are smooth and uniform.

Boil. To cook at a liquid boiling temperature, 212°F. at sea level. When boiling a liquid, bubbles will form rapidly, rise continually, and break as they reach the surface of the liquid.

Braise. To brown meat quickly in fat, cook it in a covered pan on the stovetop or in the oven.

Bread. To coat a raw food with bread crumbs. Such crumbs are often mixed with a beaten egg, or the food is first dipped in the beaten egg and then coated with bread crumbs.

Broil. To cook food by placing it on a rack that is directly under a source of heat.

Pan broil. To cook food in a heavy ungreased pan on top of the stove. Grease from the food is poured off while cooking so that the food does not fry.

Chill. To place food in the refrigerator for several hours until cold throughout.

Chop. To cut food in pieces about the size of small peas.

Cool. To remove food from the source of heat and let stand at room temperature. Do not put food in the refrigerator in an attempt to bring the temperature down more quickly.

Cream. To mix one or more ingredients until creamy and soft.

Cut in. To use a knife or pastry blender to add shortening or butter to dry ingredients until it forms small particles.

Dice. To cut food into small uniform cubes.

Dredge. To coat raw meat with a dry mixture, usually flour or cornmeal, prior to frying.

Fold in. To add a new ingredient gently to an already-beaten mixture. The new ingredient is poured on top of the mixture. With a large spoon, the new ingredient is gently brought down through the middle of the mixture, and the mixture is scraped off the bottom and brought to the top. The procedure is often used to add egg whites, berries, or other fruit to batter.

Fricassee. To braise small individual serving pieces of meat or poultry in broth or sauce.

Fry. To cook food in hot fat or oil. No water is added, and no cover is used. To pan fry, food is cooked in a small amount of oil in a frying pan. To deep-fry, food is cooked in a large kettle that contains enough hot fat to cover the food or allow it to float.

Glaze. To cover a food with a mixture that hardens, adds flavor, and makes the food glossy.

Grate. To cut food into fine particles using a grater.

Grill. To cook food on a rack directly under or over the source of heat.

Knead. To make a dough or dough like substance smooth and elastic by folding, stretching, and pressing continuously until it reaches the desired texture. (When fondant for candies is kneaded, it gets satiny rather than elastic.)

Marinate. To make foods more flavorful or tender by letting them stand in liquid for several hours or overnight. The food is completely covered. Most marinades consist of cooking oil and vinegar or lemon juice with spices added for flavor.

Mince. To chop food into very fine small pieces.

Mix. To stir ingredients until they are well blended.

Parboil. To partially cook a food in boiling liquid.

Poach. To simmer in hot liquid slowly. Poaching should be a gentle process, and food should hold its shape.

Pot-roast. To brown a roast or another large piece of meat in fat quickly, then cook it in a covered pan in the oven or on top of the stove. A small amount of liquid is usually added to make the roast more tender.

Puree. To blend a cooked fruit or vegetable until it is smooth and uniform.

Roast. To cook a food, usually meat, in the oven, uncovered, without added liquid.

Sauté. To cook food quickly in melted butter until it is tender. Chopped onions are cooked until transparent.

Scald. To heat liquid to just below the boiling point.

Scallop. To cook a food in a sauce. Many scalloped foods are cooked in a cheese or cream sauce and topped with browned bread or cracker crumbs.

Sear. To brown meat rapidly by using extremely high heat.

Shred. To cut food into narrow, long pieces with a grater.

Simmer. To cook food in hot liquid just below the boiling point, usually between 185 and 210°F. Bubbles will form slowly, but break just before reaching the liquid's surface.

Soft peaks. To beat egg whites or cream until the peaks hold their shape but droop slightly when beaters are lifted out of the bowl.

Steam. To cook with steam, food is put on a rack or in a perforated pan and placed in a covered container with a small amount of boiling water in the bottom. The steam from the boiling water cooks the food.

Steep. To simmer food in liquid below the boiling point over an extended period of time.

Stew. To simmer food slowly in liquid for several hours.

Stiff peaks. To beat egg whites or cream until the peaks stand up straight without dropping when beaters are lifted out of the bowl.

Stir. To combine two or more ingredients thoroughly, using a circular motion, generally with a spoon.

Whip. To beat a food rapidly so that air is added to it. Whipping will increase the volume but lighten the consistency of the food.

Cooking Tips

Baking Hints

When using raisins or berries, put them in a paper bag with flour and shake to coat, then they will not sink to the bottom of the batter during baking.

To keep cake from sticking, take out of the oven and put the pan on a wet towel to cool. (Do not do this with glass baking dishes.)

When baking bread, put a dish of water in the oven during baking to keep the crust soft.

To reheat biscuits, put them in a brown paper sack and twist it closed, then sprinkle the sack generously with water. Place the sack in the oven and bake at 350°F. for five minutes.

When melting chocolate, grease the pan it is melting in and the chocolate will not stick.

To cut marshmallow, rub butter on scissors.

To form popcorn balls, rub butter on hands.

Grating and Slicing

Chill cheese before grating.

Nut breads and raw meats slice easily when partially frozen.

Meatloaf is easier to slice if you wait ten minutes after taking it out of the oven before cutting it.

Freshly baked bread is easier to slice when placed on its side.

Egg and Dairy

To keep hard-boiled eggs from cracking during cooking, gently submerge them in cold water, add a teaspoon of salt to the water, and let them heat slowly to boiling. If the shell does happen to crack, add some vinegar to the water as the eggs cook to seal the crack.

After cooking, put hard-boiled eggs (still in the pan) under cold running water before removing the shells.

To store egg yolks, cover them with a mixture of cold water and a teaspoon of salad oil, then keep them in the refrigerator.

Soups, Stews, and Sauces

When using flour to thicken a liquid, sprinkle the flour with salt first and the liquid will not turn lumpy.

To thicken soup or stew, use instant mashed potato flakes, stir in ¼ to ½ cup until soup reaches desired consistency.

To absorb the grease in soup or stew, drop in a clean leaf of lettuce. Remove the lettuce when the cooking is finished.

If the soup or stew is too salty, add equal amounts of sugar and vinegar, or add chunks of raw potato. Remove potato before serving (it will have absorbed the salt).

Meat and Poultry

To make juicy hamburgers, place a chip of ice on top of the patty just as it begins to cook.

To cut down baking time for meatloaf, bake in single-serving size muffin tins or mini loaf pans.

For juicier chicken, bake with the skin on to seal in juices, then remove the skin before serving.

For crispy chicken, rub the skin with mayonnaise before broiling.

To keep roast beef from drying out when reheating, simmer in broth in a saucepan. If the roast is not heated all the way through, slice it, arrange the pieces on an ovenproof plate, and return it to the oven for ten to fifteen minutes.

Tasty Vegetables

When submerging spinach, beet greens, lettuce, or other greens in water to wash, put a handful of salt in the water remove the grit. Rinse thoroughly with clear water afterward.

When boiling cauliflower, add a small amount of milk to the water to keep the vegetable white.

When boiling vegetables, add a teaspoon of sugar to enhance natural flavors.

Instead of boiling beets, bake them in the oven like potatoes.

To speed up baking time for potatoes, soak them in salt water for 30 minutes before baking or cut the potatoes in half lengthwise and place them cut side down on a greased or buttered baking sheet. Bake for 35 minutes at 425°F.

Kitchen Tips

To clean a glass oven door, sprinkle baking soda onto a damp cloth, use circular motions to wipe the entire door. The soda will dissolve baked-on stains. Rinse with clean water and wipe dry.

To clean a food spill in the oven, sprinkle with salt while the spill is still hot. When oven cools, scrape off with a spatula.

To extinguish small stovetop fires, keep a box of baking soda or a container of salt nearby and pour over flames.

To keep stains off an oven floor and the covers under stove burners, line with foil. When the foil gets dirty, discard and replace with new.

If you do not have hot water to rinse dishes, dip the dishes in a solution of one gallon of cold water and ¼ cup of liquid bleach. Wipe dishes thoroughly with a clean towel.

To get a raw egg off the floor, cover it with salt, wait five minutes, and it will easily sweep up.

To remove coffee and tea stains from countertops, cups and fabric, rub with a paste made of baking soda and water.

To clean burned pans, coat area with paste of baking soda and water. Let stand for three hours then scrape with a plastic spatula.

For a shiny floor, add a cup of vinegar to mop water.

Granny's Favorite

Breakfast Recipes

Soft and Hard boiled eggs....page 2

The Deedol Collection...

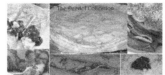

Swedish Pancakes... page 5

French Toast... page 10

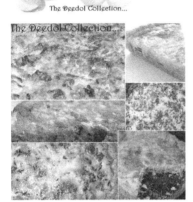

Quiche Lorraine... page 3

Easy Fried Eggs

2 eggs

1 tbsp. water

1 tbsp. butter

salt and pepper to taste

Melt butter in frying pan on medium heat. Break the eggs and slip them into the hot butter. Reduce the heat to low. Spoon melted butter over eggs periodically as they cook. Season with salt and pepper to taste.

A firmly cooked fried egg takes about 10 minutes to cook on the stove. For less fat, coat pan with nonsticking cooking spray. Cook eggs until whites are firm on the bottom. Add water to pan and cover to steam. Cook until yokes are preferred soft, medium, or hard.

1

Scrambled Eggs

2 eggs per serving   3 tbsp. milk per serving
2 tbsp. butter   salt and pepper to taste
shredded cheese (optional)

Melt butter in frying pan on medium heat. In a bowl, break eggs, add milk and spices, beat together, and pour into hot frying pan. Stir so the uncooked portion runs to the bottom of the pan. Continue this process for 3 to 5 minutes or until eggs are completely cooked. Add cheese to melt during last few minutes of cooking.

Soft-Boiled Eggs

In a saucepan, put eggs and fill with cold water 2 inches above eggs. Bring water to a rapid boil, cover pan, and remove from heat. Let stand for 2 minutes. Drain water and fill pan with cold water. Cool eggs slightly. Peel egg and serve with salt and pepper. Or break shelled eggs in half with a knife and scoop out soft egg with a spoon.

Hard-Boiled Eggs

In a saucepan, put eggs and fill with cold water about 2 inches above eggs. Bring water to a rapid boil. Cover pan and remove from heat. Let stand for 15 to 20 minutes. Drain water and fill pan with cold water to cool eggs. Break, peel eggs, and rinse with cold water. Serve with salt and pepper.

Poached Eggs

Fill a saucepan with water. Heat water to boiling and reduce heat to low. One at a time, break eggs and slip gently into simmering water. Cook eggs until firm, about 4 to 5 minutes. Add salt and pepper to taste during cooking time. Remove with slotted spoon. Drain each egg on paper towels and serve with toast or biscuit.

Fried Egg Sandwich

2 eggs
2 slices cheddar cheese
mayonnaise

1 pickle
2 slices bread
salt and pepper to taste

Fry eggs in bacon fat until yolks are hard and edges of egg are crispy. One minute before eggs are done, add salt, pepper, and cheese so it melts on top. Toast bread. Slice pickle. Apply mayo to toast and put eggs and cheese on top of one slice, add pickles, and top with second piece of toast.

Easy Cheese Omelet

1 tbsp. butter
3 eggs, beaten
1 ½ cups cheddar cheese

salt and pepper to taste
1 tbsp. milk

Melt butter in frying pan. Beat together, eggs, salt, pepper, and milk until fluffy. Pour into hot pan and cook over medium heat. When eggs are still glossy, sprinkle cheese on top. Fold in half. Serve Immediately. Try other stuffing, including cooked bacon or ham, onions, mushrooms, green peppers, or fresh avocado. Granny's favorite is with all the above.

Quiche Lorraine

9-inch pie shell, baked
6 slices bacon, cooked and crumbled
1 cup swiss cheese, shredded
6 eggs, beaten
dash of nutmeg

1 cup milk
½ tsp. salt
dash of pepper
chives

Preheat oven to 350°F. Sprinkle bacon and cheese in bottom of pie shell. Combine remaining ingredients in small bowl. Mix well and pour over bacon and cheese. Sprinkle with chives. Bake for 30 to 40 minutes or until knife inserted in center comes out clean. Let stand for 5 to 10 minutes before cutting. As a variation, try a totally veggie quiche with broccoli, onion, green peppers, tomatoes, mushrooms, or any of your favorite veggies.

Easy Oven Omelet

4 eggs

½ cup milk

salt and pepper to taste

½ pkg. sliced corned beef (about 3 oz.)

½ cup cheese, grated

1 ½ tsp. onion, grated

Preheat oven to 325°F. Beat eggs, milk, and seasonings together. Tear corned beef into small pieces. Add to egg mixture. Stir in cheese and onion. Pour into greased baking pan. Bake for 20 to 30 minutes or until eggs are set.

Quick Quiche

3 slices bacon, cooked and crumbled

1 cup grated cheese

½ cup chopped onions

4 eggs

2 cups milk

½ cup biscuit mix (see p. 93)

½ tsp. salt

dash of pepper

Preheat oven to 350°F. Grease pie plate. Sprinkle bacon, cheese, and onions over bottom. Beat eggs and milk together. Add remaining ingredients. Beat until well mixed. Pour into pie plate. Bake for 50 to 55 minutes or until knife inserted in center comes out clean. Let stand 5 to 10 minutes before cutting.

Scratch Pancake

2 eggs, well beaten

½ cup milk

2 tbsp. cooking oil

bacon fat to grease griddle

2 tsp. baking powder

½ tsp. salt

¾ cup flour

½ tsp. sugar (optional)

Sift together flour, baking powder, salt, and sugar in bowl. In another bowl, beat together eggs, milk, and oil. Stir egg mixture into flour mixture until all ingredients are well blended. Pour onto greased griddle or frying pan. Cook until pancake bubbles slightly, then turn and cook other side until golden brown. Top with favorite butter and syrup or jam. Granny's favorite is peanut butter and apricot syrup.

Swedish Pancakes

3 eggs   1 tbsp. sugar
1 ¼ cups milk   ½ tsp. salt
¾ cup sifted flour

Combine ingredients in a bowl and beat with wire whip. Cook thin pancakes on medium heat until golden brown on both sides. Serve with favorite topping.

Applesauce Roll Pancakes

2 eggs, well beaten   ½ cup milk
½ cup flour   ½ tsp. salt
1 tbsp. sugar, optional   1 cup applesauce
powdered sugar, optional

Heat applesauce in a saucepan until warm. Mix eggs and milk in medium bowl. Add flour, salt, and sugar. Beat until smooth. Grease small frying pan and heat until very hot. Pour ¼ of batter into pan. Tip pan quickly until batter covers bottom. Turn and brown on other side. Remove from pan, spread with ¼ cup warm applesauce, and roll. Sprinkle with powdered sugar, if desired. Granny does not need any sugar; she is sweet enough already.

German Pancakes

6 eggs	¼ tsp. salt
1 cup milk	4 tbsp. butter
1 cup flour	2 pie pans

Preheat oven to 450°F. Combine eggs, milk, flour, and salt in a bowl. Beat until fluffy and smooth. Put 2 tbsp. of butter in each pie pan and put pans into preheated oven. When butter is melted, remove from oven and pour half of the batter in each pan and bake for 20 minutes or until puffy and golden brown.

Moist Oatmeal Pancakes

2 cups quick-cooking oatmeal	2 eggs, beaten
1 ½ cups milk	dash of salt
½ cup granulated sugar	¼ tsp. cinnamon
1 tsp. baking powder	dash of nutmeg

Mix ingredients in a large bowl. Beat until batter is thin; if batter is too thick, add a little more milk. Heat a greased griddle and pour the pancakes. Cook until bubbles are seen and the edges are dry. Flip over with a spatula, and cook until golden brown. Top with favorite syrup or jam.

Potato Pancakes

2 eggs	dash of nutmeg
1 tbsp. flour	2 grated potatoes
½ tsp. salt	4 slices bacon, cooked and crumbled
2 tsp. minced onion	1 cup warm applesauce

Combine eggs, flour, salt, onion, nutmeg, bacon, and potatoes. Pour one-fourth of mixture into hot greased frying pan, one pancake at a time. Makes 4. Cook on both sides until golden brown. Spoon warm applesauce over the top of each potato pancake or serve on the side.

Whole Wheat Pancakes

2/3 cup whole wheat flour	1 egg, beaten
1 ½ tsp. baking powder	2/3 cup milk
4 tsp. granulated sugar	4 tsp. cooking oil
¼ tsp. baking soda	

Combine dry ingredients in a bowl. Combine egg, milk, and oil in another bowl. Stir in flour mixture. Pour batter onto hot, ungreased frying pan. Cook until golden brown. Serve with favorite topping.

Easy Waffles

1 cup flour	1 cup milk
1 tsp. baking powder	2 tsp. lemon juice or vinegar
¼ tsp. salt	2 tbsp. butter
¼ tsp. baking soda	1 egg, beaten

Combine dry ingredients in a bowl. Stir in milk, lemon juice, butter, and egg. Cook in greased waffle iron. Serve with favorite topping.

Easy Maple Syrup

2 cups granulated sugar
½ tsp. maple extract
1 cup water

Bring sugar and water to a boil and remove from heat. Stir in extract and serve over your favorite pancakes.

Brown Sugar Syrup

1 cup packed brown sugar	1 tbsp. butter
½ cup water	½ tsp. vanilla extract

Bring sugar and water to a boil for 2 minutes. Remove from heat and stir in butter and vanilla. Serve warm.

Creamy Cinnamon Syrup

½ cup light corn syrup	1 tsp. cinnamon
1 cup granulated sugar	½ cup evaporated milk
¼ cup water	

Bring corn syrup, sugar, water, and cinnamon to a boil. Cook 2 to 3 minutes. Allow to cool for 5 minutes. Stir in milk and serve warm.

Honey Maple Syrup

¾ cup granulated sugar	½ cup butter
½ cup light corn syrup	¼ tsp. maple extract

Combine ingredients in a saucepan and cook, stirring occasionally until butter is melted and sugar dissolves. Serve warm or cold.

Applesauce

4 large apples (Jonathan and McIntosh)	¼ cup granulated sugar
1 tsp. cinnamon	1 dash of nutmeg
4 tbsp. water	

In a saucepan, put peeled, cored, and chopped apples in with the water. In a small bowl, mix sugar and spices. When apples are cooked to tender (about

20 minutes), add sugar mixture and stir frequently. Cook for 10 to 15 more minutes or until applesauce is the consistency you prefer. Serve warm.

Nutty Granola

4 cups quick-cooking oatmeal

1 ½ cups shredded coconut

1 cup sunflower seeds

2 cups walnuts, chopped

1 cup cooking oil

½ cup water

2 tsp. vanilla extract

Preheat oven to 275°F. Combine ingredients and spread on a cookie sheet. Bake for 2 hours, stirring often. Serve with milk.

Easy Granola

3 ½ cups quick-cooking oats

¼ cup cooking oil

¼ cup honey

1 tbsp. vanilla extract

½ cup packed brown sugar

½ cup chopped nuts

Combine all ingredients and spread on cookie sheet. Bake in preheated oven at 300°F. Serve with milk and shredded coconut if desired.

Plum Clafouti

¼ cup plus 1 tbsp. sugar

¾ lb. Italian prunes, halved and pitted

2 eggs

1 egg yolk

1 tsp. vanilla

¾ cup milk

¾ cup cream

¾ cup flour

1/8 tsp. salt

vanilla sugar, for sprinkling

Preheat oven to 400°F. Butter baking dish well. Sprinkle the dish with sugar and put the plum halves over the sugar, skin side down. In a blender, blend the milk, cream, flour, eggs, egg yolk, and salt for 2 minutes. Mix sugar and vanilla; add ¼ cup to batter, mix a few seconds, and pour over plums. Bake the clafouti in the middle of the oven for 30 minutes or until puffed and golden. Dust the clafouti with remaining vanilla sugar and serve at once.

Baked Breakfast Surprise

2 lbs. shredded potatoes	1 small onion chopped
6 eggs, beaten	2 cups chopped ham
1 chopped bell pepper	½ cup milk
any chopped veggies	1 cup shredded cheese
salt and pepper to taste	dash of garlic powder

Preheat oven to 425°F. Mix potatoes, onion, ham, bell peppers, and any other veggies you might find in the fridge. In a small bowl, beat eggs, milk, and spices together and add to potato mixture. Toss to coat. Put in baking dish, and bake for 20 minutes. Add shredded cheese on top, and bake for additional 10 minutes.

"The way to a man's heart is through his stomach."

French Toast

4 eggs, beaten	½ cup milk
4 slices bread	sugar and cinnamon mixed

Preheat griddle to 350°F. Whip eggs and milk together in a pie plate. Dip bread into egg mixture and place on hot greased griddle, all 4 slices, one at a time. Pour remaining egg mixture on top of cooking bread to use up. Sprinkle with sugar and cinnamon mixture. Turn and cook on other side until golden brown. Top with butter.

Oatmeal (Grandpa's Favorite)

1 ½ cups water
¾ cup quick-cooking oats
¼ to ½ cup Granny's applesauce

1 large pinch of salt
1 tbsp. butter
½ cup milk or cream

In a saucepan, put water and salt. Bring to a boil and add oats. Bring to a boil for 5 minutes. Remove from heat and add butter, applesauce, and milk. Makes 1 serving. Serve immediately.

Biscuits and Gravy

2 cups sifted flour
1 tsp. salt
1/3 cup shortening

1 tbsp. baking powder
¾ cup milk (add ¼ cup for drop biscuits)

Sift together dry ingredients. Cut in shortening until crumbly. Add milk until dough forms. Roll out dough and cut biscuits (or drop by heaping spoonful) onto greased baking sheet; bake at 375°F. for 15 minutes or until golden brown.

Gravy

½ cup butter (1 stick)
salt and pepper to taste

½ cup flour
2 cups milk

For gravy, put butter into frying pan and melt until bubbling. Whip together milk, flour, and spices until foamy. Add to melted butter, stirring constantly. Bring to a boil, stirring constantly for 5 minutes or until gravy starts to thicken. Remove from heat and set to cool. Gravy will thicken while cooling. Pour over biscuits and serve. Serves 4.

Granny's Favorite
Lunch Recipes

  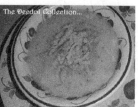

Tuna Melts... page 13   *Chicken and Dumplings...*   *Clam Chowder... page 18*
                            page 16

Top Ramen Surprise

1 pkg. Top Ramen   2 eggs
¼ cup shredded cheddar cheese   6 sliced black olives

Fill hot water just over ramen noodles in a saucepan and add raw eggs. Bring to a boil and add noodle spices, olives, and cheese. Cook until cheese is melted. Remove from heat to cool for 5 minutes and serve immediately.

Peanut Butter and Jelly Sandwich

2 slices bread   1 tbsp. peanut butter
1 tbsp. jam or jelly

Apply peanut butter to both slices of bread. Smooth on jelly to 1 slice of bread and put bread together. Slice and serve.

Tuna Salad Sandwich

1 can drained tuna   2 tbsp. mayonnaise
1 dill pickle, chopped   1/8 cup chopped onion
1 stalk celery, chopped   salt and pepper to taste

Combine all ingredients and mix well. Smooth mixture onto between 2 slices of bread. Makes 4 sandwiches.

Tuna Melts

2 slices bread
2 slices cheese
2 tbsp. mayonnaise

1 tbsp. butter
1 can drained tuna
salt and pepper to taste

Mix together, tuna, mayo, and spices. Butter outside of each slice of bread; place cheese and tuna mixture between. Heat on hot griddle until both sides are golden brown and cheese is melted. Serves 1.

Egg Salad Sandwich

4 hard-boiled eggs, chopped
salt and pepper to taste

2 tbsp. mayonnaise
4 slices bread

Combine eggs, mayo, and spices and mix well. Spread on 2 slices of bread, and cover with the other 2 slices. Serves 2.

Ingredients that can be added for a variation are chopped celery, dill pickle, onion.

Grilled Cheese Sandwich and Tomato Soup

4 slices bread
4 tbsp. butter
8 slices cheese (cheddar or Velveeta)

Heat griddle to 325°F. Butter one side of each bread slice. Place butter side down onto griddle and place 2 slices of cheese on each bread. Cover with other 2 bread slices, butter side out. Grill both sides until golden brown or cheese is melted through. Heat tomato soup with 1 can of milk until hot. Dip sandwich in soup and eat. One of Granny's most favorites.

Rueben Sandwich

4 slices bread	2 tbsp. Thousand Island dressing
6 slices corned beef	½ cup sauerkraut
4 tbsp. butter	4 slices swiss cheese

Heat griddle to 325°F. Butter one side of each bread slice. Place butter side down onto griddle and place 2 slices swiss cheese on 2 bread slices on griddle. Top with 3 slices of corned beef and ¼ cup sauerkraut, 1 tbsp. Dressing, and other buttered bread slice on each sandwich. Grill on each side until all is melted and heated through.

Hoagie Sandwich

2 hoagie buns	4 slices ham
4 slices turkey	4 slices bologna
2 tbsp. mayonnaise	2 tbsp. mustard
6 slices onion	2 sliced dill pickles
2 slices swiss cheese	2 slices cheddar cheese
4 sliced black olives	4 slices tomato
lettuce torn into leaves	salt and pepper to taste

Split hoagie buns. Spread mayo and mustard on each bun, and sprinkle salt and pepper on buns. On each, layer cheese, meats, tomato, onion, pickle, olives, and lettuce.

Beans and Franks

2 hot dog buns	2 hot dogs
1 tbsp. mustard	1 tbsp. ketchup
1 small can pork and beans	1 cup cottage cheese

Toast hot dog buns. Place cooked hot dogs on each bun. Apply mustard and ketchup on each side of buns. On the side, place pork and beans and top with cottage cheese.

Franks with Macaroni and Cheese

1 cup macaroni noodles (dry)   Velveeta cheese
1 pkg. hot dogs   2 tbsp. butter
salt and pepper to taste   1/3 cup milk

Cook noodles until tender. Add butter, Velveeta cheese, milk, and spices and mix well. Add chopped hot dogs to macaroni and cheese mixture. Heat and serve.

Hamburger Soup

1 lb. lean ground beef   1 lb. red potatoes
1 qt. stewed tomatoes   1 medium onion, chopped
1 can sweet peas   1 can green beans
beefsteak seasoning   salt and pepper to taste

Crumble and brown beef in a large soup pan. Add potatoes, stewed tomatoes, onions, peas, green beans, and seasonings. Cover with water and bring to a boil. Add gravy sauce (see below) to thicken soup. Bring to a boil and reduce heat. Stir often. Remove from heat and serve with your favorite biscuit recipe and butter.

Gravy Sauce

½ cup flour
1 cup cold water

Shake well and pour in a steady stream into soup. It will thicken real nice. Stir constantly.

Beef and Bean Chili

1 lb. lean ground beef	1 cup chopped onion
1 stalk celery, chopped	1 tsp. salt
1 tsp. sugar	1 qt. stewed tomatoes
2 tbsp. cider vinegar	2 tsp. garlic powder
2 tbsp. chili powder	2 cans kidney or pinto beans

Crumble and brown beef in a large soup pan, add onion and celery, and cook until done. Drain and add remaining ingredients and simmer for 20 minutes. Serve with corn bread (recipe in "Breads").

Beef Stew

1 lb. beef stew meat	1 tbsp. olive oil
1 lb. potato, peeled, cubed	water to cover
1 pkg. frozen vegetables	1 pkg. dry onion soup mix
2 tbsp. flour	¼ cup water

In a large stew pot, brown meat in oil, cover, and simmer until tender. Stir in soup mix, potatoes, vegetables, and water to cover all; bring to a boil. Cook on medium heat for 15 minutes. In a bowl, stir flour into ¼ cup water; blend well. Pour into stew, stirring until it thickens, then serve.

Chicken and Dumplings

1 lb. chicken, cut up	½ bay leaf
water to cover	salt and pepper to taste
1 large onion, chopped	2 cups chopped celery
1 cup chopped carrots	½ tsp. poultry seasoning

In a soup pan, put chicken, onion, seasonings, and cover with water. Cover with lid and bring to a boil. Turn heat down to simmer and cook for 2 hours. Add vegetables, and add water to cover. Bring to a boil; reduce heat to medium and cook for 20 minutes. Top with dumpling dough.

Dumplings

1 cup flour

1 ½ tsp. baking powder

2/3 cup milk

salt and pepper to taste

2 tbsp. shortening

1 egg, beaten

Stir together dry ingredients. Cut in shortening until crumbly. Mix egg and milk well and add to flour mixture. Stir only until flour is dampened. Dough will be lumpy. Drop spoonfuls on top of soup. Cover and steam for 15 minutes without lifting the lid.

Cheese Soup

2 tbsp. butter

2 tbsp. chopped celery

2 tbsp. chopped carrots

1 tbsp. chopped onion

½ tsp. salt

dash of pepper

3 tbsp. cornstarch

2 cups cold milk

2 cups grated cheddar cheese

croutons

Sauté vegetables in butter until tender. Add seasonings. Blend in cornstarch and milk together, and add to vegetables stirring constantly. Heat until thick and bubbly. Stir in cheese until melted. Top with croutons and serve.

Cream of Turkey Soup

1 tbsp. butter

½ cup chopped onion

2 cups hot water

2 chicken bouillon cubes

2 cups diced potatoes

1 cup cooked and cubed turkey

1 can carrots

1 can peas

1 tsp. salt

½ tsp. pepper

1 cup evaporated milk

Sauté onion in butter. Dissolve bouillon cubes in hot water. Add remaining ingredients except milk. Simmer for 10 minutes. Stir in milk and heat through. Do not boil.

Clam Chowder

2 lbs. potatoes, peeled and diced
½ cup onions, diced
2 stalks celery, diced
¼ cup butter

2 tbsp. flour
1 cup milk
1 small can of diced clams, drained

Cook potatoes, onions, and celery in salted boiling water until tender for about 10 minutes. Drain and mash. In separate saucepan, melt butter and stir in flour. Add milk gradually, stirring constantly until thickened. Stir in potato mixture and clams. Heat through.

Potato Soup

4 lbs. cubed potatoes
½ cup flour
water to cover
1 cup milk

1 cube butter
4 stalks diced celery
1 small chopped onion
salt and pepper to taste

Cover veggies, spices, and butter with water and cook until tender. Blend flour and milk then add to soup, stirring constantly until soup thickens.

Potato and Ham Chowder

1 tbsp. butter
¼ cup diced onion
¼ cup chopped green peppers
2 lbs. diced potatoes
1 cup water

½ tsp. salt
dash of pepper
¼ tsp. paprika
2 tbsp. flour
1 cup chopped ham

Melt butter in a large soup pan. Add onion and green pepper. Sauté until tender. Add potatoes, water, and spices. Cover and simmer about 15 minutes or until potatoes are tender. Combine flour and small amount of water into a paste and add to soup. Add milk and cook until thickened, stirring constantly. Stir in ham and heat through.

Tomato and Rice Soup

1 tbsp. butter	½ cup uncooked rice
1 cup chopped onion	1 tsp. salt
½ cup chopped celery	½ tsp. chili powder
1 large can tomatoes	3 cups water
2 beef bouillon cubes	

Sauté onion and celery in butter until tender. Add remaining ingredients and bring to a boil. Reduce heat and simmer for 20 minutes or until rice is tender. Serve immediately.

Minestrone

3 beef bouillon cubes	1 tbsp. chopped onion
2 cups boiling water	¼ tsp. salt, pepper, and basil
1 can corn	½ cup uncooked macaroni
1 can stewed tomatoes	1 can lima beans

Dissolve bouillon cubes in water in large soup pan. Add remaining ingredients. Cover and simmer about 45 minutes.

Granny's Favorite
Dinner Recipes

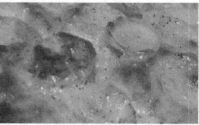

BBQ Chicken Bake... page 21   *Granny's Scalloped Potatoes... page 38*

Beef Pot Roast... page 30

Chicken Casserole

1 can cream of chicken soup

1 can cream of mushroom soup

½ cup milk

1 cup instant rice, uncooked

1 pkg. dry onion soup mix

2 lbs. cut-up chicken

Preheat oven to 325°F. Combine soups and milk stir until blended well. Sprinkle rice in 9"× 13" greased baking pan. Arrange chicken pieces on rice. Pour soup mixture over chicken and rice. Sprinkle dry soup mix over chicken. Cover with foil tightly and bake for 2 hours or until chicken is cooked through.

BBQ Chicken Bake

2 tbsp. worcestershire sauce	1 tbsp. sugar
¼ cup ketchup	1 tbsp. cider vinegar
1 tbsp. steak sauce	2 lbs. chicken thighs and legs

Preheat oven to 350°F. Combine all ingredients except chicken and mix well. Arrange chicken, skin side up, in greased baking dish. Brush generously with sauce. Bake uncovered for 1 hour.

Crock-Pot Scalloped Potatoes and Ham

2 lbs. potatoes, thinly sliced	¼ cup flour
4 tbsp. butter	2 cups diced ham
salt and pepper	2 cups grated cheddar cheese
1 small onion, chopped	1 can cream of mushroom soup

Place half of the potatoes and ham in a lightly greased Crock-Pot. Layer with half of the onions, the flour and spices; repeat for second layer. Dot the top with butter then pour the cream of mushroom soup over the top. Cover and cook on low for 7 to 9 hours. About 30 minutes before serving, sprinkle the grated cheese on top. Cook until melted.

Medley Noodle Casserole

2 tbsp. butter	½ cup diced onion
1 cup dices celery	½ cup diced green peppers
1 lb. lean ground beef	2 cups uncooked noodles
1 can red kidney beans	3 cups tomatoes
1 can button mushrooms	1 tsp. salt
1 tsp. chili powder	1/8 tsp. pepper

In large pan, melt butter and brown ground beef, onions, celery, and green peppers. Add uncooked noodles, kidney beans, tomatoes, mushroom, and seasonings. Cook on low heat for about 30 minutes.

Chicken Pot Pie

2 lbs. cooked cubed chicken	2 cups diced potatoes
1 cup diced carrots	½ cup chopped onion
½ cup chopped celery	salt and pepper to taste
½ tsp. brown sage	3 cups chicken broth
½ cup milk	¼ cup cornstarch
1 cup frozen peas	biscuits uncooked

Boil carrots, potatoes, celery, and onion until tender in salted water; drain and put in bottom of large casserole pan then top with chicken.

Gravy

In a saucepan, place broth and spices and heat. Thicken with milk and cornstarch, stirring constantly. Add the peas and pour gravy over chicken and vegetables.

Top with uncooked biscuits. Bake at 450°F or until top is golden brown. Serves 6 to 8 people.

Chicken Loaf

2 lbs. cooked chicken cubed	3 cups bread, cubed
½ cup diced onion	½ tsp. sage
¼ cup diced celery	3 eggs
3 1/2 cups chicken broth	4 tbsp. bacon drippings
little bit of flour	½ cup chicken broth
1 can mushrooms	salt and pepper to taste

Mix cubed chicken with bread, onion, sage, and celery in a greased pan. Beat 3 eggs and pour over mixture. Pour 3 cups chicken broth over mixture and bake for 45 minutes at 350°F. Serve with sauce.

Sauce

Mix well and heat bacon drippings, flour, and ½ cup chicken broth and mushrooms until thickened, salt and pepper to taste. Pour over chicken loaf and serve.

Pork Roast and Gravy

In a roasting pan, brown pork roast on all sides. Remove from stove and add just enough water to cover bottom of roasting pan. Add potatoes, onions, and carrots. Cover and roast for 2 ½ hours at 325°F. Remove veggies and roasted meat. Drain off most of the fat. Add enough water to juice to make 1 ½ cups liquid. Put ½ cup cold water in shaker and add ¼ cup flour and shake well. Stir into pan juices and cook on top of stove in roasting pan, stirring constantly until gravy is thick and bubbly. Salt and pepper to taste. Simmer for 2 to 3 minutes. Makes 2 cups gravy.

Mashed Potatoes with Onions Casserole

4 cups mashed potatoes	6 eggs, beaten
3 cups shredded cheddar cheese	½ cup milk
½ chopped small onion	

Mix and bake at 375°F for 50 minutes.

Zucchini Egg Foo Yung

3 cup grated zucchini	3 eggs, beaten
¼ tsp. garlic salt	¼ cup flour

Mix all ingredients and drop by tablespoon into hot oil in a skillet. Brown on both sides and serve with chicken or pork gravy.

Beef Stroganoff

½ cup minced onion
¼ cup butter
2 tbsp. flour
1 small can sliced mushrooms
1 cup sour cream

1 clove garlic, minced
1 lb. lean ground beef
1 tsp. salt
1 can cream of chicken soup

Sauté onion and garlic in butter over medium heat. Add meat and brown. Add flour, salt, pepper, and mushrooms. Cook for 5 minutes and add soup. Simmer uncovered for 10 minutes. Stir in sour cream. Heat through, and serve with noodles or rice. Serves 4 to 6.

Egg Noodles

3 eggs
2 ½ cup sifted flour

1 tsp. melted butter

Use all the flour. Beat eggs lightly and add butter. Stir in flour gradually. Use all flour for cutting into strips. (Use less flour for ravioli recipe.)
Turn stiff dough onto lightly floured board. Roll very thinly into stiff sheets. Spread out onto lightly floured cloths to dry. Before the sheets of dough are too stiff to handle, fold over 2 or 3 times and cut into thin shreds. Toss the shreds apart to dry thoroughly. Keep in tightly closed glass jar until ready to use.

Asparagus Chicken Casserole

2 lbs. fresh asparagus spears
4 boneless chicken breasts
2 tbsp. olive oil
1 can cream of mushroom soup
½ cup mayonnaise

1 tsp. lemon juice
½ tsp. curry powder
¼ tsp. garlic powder
¼ tsp. onion salt
1 cup Colby-Jack cheese, grated

Preheat oven to 375°F. Partially steam asparagus. Place asparagus in greased 9"× 13" baking pan. Set aside. In frying pan, brown chicken in oil. Place chicken over asparagus. In bowl, mix soup, mayonnaise, lemon juice, and spices. Pour over chicken. Cover and bake for 30 minutes. Remove from oven and sprinkle with cheese. Bake in oven uncovered for 10 minutes or until chicken juices run clear.

Meat Loaf

1 lb. lean ground beef	2 eggs, beaten
1 cup oatmeal	½ cup chopped onion
½ cup chopped celery	½ cup chopped tomatoes
½ cup chopped green pepper	1 shredded carrot
3 tbsp. ketchup	chili powder, salt, and pepper

Mix well with your hands the ground beef with the veggies and oatmeal and place in loaf pan. Top with ketchup and spices. Bake at 400°F for 40 to 45 minutes.

Basic Gravy

4 tbsp. meat drippings or butter	2 cups milk or cream
4 tbsp. flour	spice to taste

Combine drippings and flour, stirring over medium heat until smooth. Stirring constantly, add heated milk and salt and pepper to taste. If butter is used, add onion, celery, and garlic powder for extra flavor.

Quick Gravy

meat drippings
1 can condensed cream of chicken, mushroom or celery soup
Milk

In a skillet, bring meat drippings to a boil. Reduce heat and add soup. Add milk to desired consistency.

For chicken, use cream of chicken soup; for beef or ham, use cream of mushroom soup; and for pork, use cream of celery soup.

Beef and Noodles

1 lb. lean ground beef	1 pkg. dry onion soup mix
¼ cup fresh parsley, chopped	4 cups hot water
1 cup carrots, chopped	1 cup noodles, uncooked
½ cup celery, chopped	2 small tomatoes, chopped

Brown beef and drain off the grease. Stir in parsley, carrots, celery, soup mix and water. Bring to a boil. Reduce heat and simmer for 15 minutes, stirring occasionally. Add noodles. Cover and cook until tender, about 10 minutes. Add tomatoes and heat through.

Meatballs

1 lb. lean ground beef	1 pkg. dry onion soup mix
½ cup water	2 tbsp. flour
¼ cup cracker crumbs	½ tsp. garlic powder
2 eggs, beaten	2 small tomatoes, chopped
1 tbsp. cooking oil	½ cup sour cream

Combine beef, half of the soup mix, cracker crumbs, and eggs. Form into meatballs and brown in hot oil. In a bowl, combine remaining soup mix, water, flour, garlic powder, tomatoes, and sour cream. Pour into pan over meatballs. Cover and simmer for 10 minutes.

Beef Rolls and Gravy

½ lb. lean ground beef

½ cup onion, chopped

¼ cup ketchup

1 tbsp. worcestershire sauce

¼ tsp. pepper

2 cups biscuit mix (see p. 93)

2/3 cup milk

2 tbsp. flour

3 cup hot water

2 beef bouillon cubes

Preheat oven to 475°F. Brown beef in frying pan. Add onions and cook until tender. Stir in ketchup, worcestershire sauce, and pepper. Take mixtures out of pan and set aside. In a bowl, combine biscuit mix and milk. Knead into rectangles. Spread with meat mixture. Roll up and pinch seams shut. Slice into one-inch-thick rounds. Arrange slices on cookie sheet. Bake for 10 minutes. In pan with drippings, stir in flour. Dissolve bouillon cubes in hot water and pour into pan. Cook, stirring constantly until thickened. Season with salt and pepper. Pour gravy over beef rolls and serve.

Tamale Pie Casserole

½ lb. lean ground beef

½ cup minced onion

2 tsp. garlic powder

8 oz. can tomato sauce

1 egg, beaten

½ cup milk

6 oz. can whole-kernel corn

¼ cup sliced black olives

½ cup cornmeal

1 tsp. chili powder

1 tsp. salt

Preheat oven to 350°F. Cook beef and onion with garlic powder. Combine tomato sauce, milk, egg, corn, olives, cornmeal, chili powder, and salt. Pour into meat and mix well. Spoon into 8"× 8" baking pan and bake for 40 to 45 minutes or until knife inserted in middle comes out clean. Cut into squares and serve.

Beef Nachos

1 lbs. lean ground beef

1 cup black olives, sliced

1 can refried beans

1 pkg. corn tortilla chips

1 small can sliced mushrooms

1/4 cup hot water

1 small onion, chopped

2 tomatoes, chopped

1 tsp. salt

1 pkg. taco seasoning

2 cups shredded cheddar cheese

1 cup green olives, chopped

Preheat oven to 400°F. In a frying pan, brown beef and add taco seasoning and water. Simmer for 15 minutes. Drain and set aside. On a baking sheet, spread a thick layer of corn tortilla chips. Top with beef then onions, olives, mushrooms, tomatoes, refried beans, and finally the cheddar cheese. Bake for 15 minutes or until cheese is melted. Serve.

Quesadillas

1/2 cup shredded cheddar cheese

½ cup shredded Monterey Jack cheese

2 tbsp. minced onion

4 flour tortillas

salsa

sour cream

In a bowl, combine cheeses and onion. Place one tortilla in lightly greased pan. Top with half of cheese mixture and some salsa. Place another tortilla on top. Brown one side. Flip to brown other side until cheese melts. Garnish with sour cream and more salsa. Repeat with second quesadilla and serve.

Spaghetti Sauce

1 lb. lean ground beef

1 can tomato sauce

1 qt. stewed tomatoes

1 pkg. spaghetti seasoning (see p. 227)

In large pot, brown beef; add stewed tomatoes (Granny stews her tomatoes with onions, celery, sweet peppers), tomato sauce, and seasonings. Bring to a boil and simmer for 2 hours. Serve with cooked spaghetti noodles.

Enchiladas

½ lb. lean ground beef

¼ cup chopped onion

2 tsp. green chilies, chopped

1 small can tomato sauce

¼ cup sliced black olives

2 cups cheddar cheese, shredded

1 can mild enchilada sauce

3 corn tortillas

½ cup sour cream

½ head shredded lettuce

Preheat oven to 350°F. In large skillet, brown beef, onion, and chilies. Stir in tomato sauce, olives, and one cup cheese. In small skillet, warm enchilada sauce with small amount of cooking oil. Place tortillas separately in sauce and turn until pliable. Pull out with tongs directly onto platter. Place spoonful of meat on each tortilla and roll up and place in a greased baking pan, seam side down. Pour enchilada sauce over tortillas and top with remaining cheese. Bake for 20 to 25 minutes. Serve with sour cream on a bed of lettuce.

Pizza

1 cup flour

½ tsp. salt

¼ tsp. pepper

2 eggs, beaten

2/3 cup milk

1 lb. lean ground beef

4 oz. can mushrooms, drained

8 oz. tomato sauce

½ tsp. oregano flakes

2 cups mozzarella cheese, shredded

In a bowl, beat flour, salt, pepper, eggs, and milk. Pour into baking pan. Brown beef and drain. Distribute beef over batter. Top with mushrooms then tomato sauce. Sprinkle with oregano flakes and top with cheese. Bake at 425°F for 20 to 25 minutes and serve.

Beef Pot Roast

3 lb. beef roast	1 onion, sliced thick
salt and pepper to taste	4 carrots, sliced thick
2 stalks celery, sliced thick	½ cup hot water
1 pkg. dry onion soup mix	3 tbsp. flour
2 lbs. red potatoes	

Brown roast on all sides in roasting pan on top of the stove, high heat. Preheat oven to 350°F. Add water to roast, just enough to coat bottom of pan. Roast beef for 1 ½ hours then add spuds. Roast for 15 minutes and add carrots. Roast for 15 minutes, and add onions on top of roast beef. Roast for 45 minutes, and take veggies out of roasting pan and set aside. Place meat on platter. In a jar, mix ½ cup hot water and flour until well blended. Pour into meat juices in roasting pan over medium heat. Cook until gravy thickens and serve.

Fried Fish

4 fish fillets, cod, red snapper, trout	salt and pepper to taste
cornmeal	olive oil with garlic

Sprinkle salt and pepper over fish fillets and roll in cornmeal until covered well. Place in hot skillet with spiced olive oil. Fry until crisp and golden brown on both sides.

BBQ Pork Ribs

BBQ sauce (see pp. 213-214)
pork ribs
salt and pepper to taste

Sprinkle salt and pepper over ribs and place on broiler pan. Apply BBQ sauce and place into preheated oven at 400°F. Turn over in 20 minutes, and apply BBQ sauce and return to oven for 20 minutes or until ribs are crispy.

Salmon Patties

½ cup flaked salmon

2 tbsp. butter

1 tbsp. flour

¼ cup milk

¼ cup bread crumbs

¼ tsp. lemon juice

1/8 tsp. salt

dash of black pepper and red pepper

Drain salmon well. In small saucepan, melt butter and stir in flour. Gradually beat in milk, stirring constantly until thickened. Add salmon, bread crumbs, lemon juice, salt, and both peppers. Form into patties with hands, let rest for 15 minutes to firm up. Sauté patties in melted butter or olive oil until lightly browned and heated through.

Potato Patties

2 cups mashed potatoes

1 slightly beaten egg

¼ cup chopped onion

salt and pepper to taste

flour

Mix potatoes, egg, onion, and spices well. Shape into 6 patties and dip in flour; then brown slowly in butter, about 5 minutes on each side. You can add garlic or other spices to taste.

Tuna Noodle Casserole

1 can tuna, drained and flaked

¾ cup mayonnaise

salt and pepper to taste

1 can peas, drained

2 cups cooked noodles

2 tbsp. lemon juice

saltine crackers

Combine all ingredients except crackers. Place in baking dish and cover with crushed crackers. Bake at 350°F for 20 minutes, covered. May be topped with shredded cheese for variation. Uncover and bake for 10 minutes.

Scalloped Tuna and Potatoes

3 tbsp. butter

3 tbsp. minced onion

½ tsp. salt

dash of pepper

3 tbsp. flour

2 cups milk

1 small can tuna, drained and flaked

3 large potatoes, thinly sliced

½ cup cheddar cheese, shredded

Sauté onion in butter until tender. Stir in salt, pepper, and flour. Whip in milk to make sauce. Continue cooking stirring, constantly until thickened. Add tuna and ¼ cup cheese. Heat through. Layer potato slices in 8"× 8" baking dish. Pour tuna mixture over potatoes. Bake covered at 350°F for 1 hour; uncover and bake for 30 minutes. Spread remaining cheese and bake until melted.

Corn Dogs

½ cup flour

¾ tsp. baking powder

1/3 cup cornmeal

1 tbsp. sugar

½ tsp. salt

½ cup milk

1 egg, beaten

1 tbsp. cooking oil

4 to 6 hot dogs

4 to 6 wooden sticks

Sift together flour, baking powder, cornmeal, sugar, and salt. Stir together milk, egg, and oil. Beat in dry ingredients. Skewer each hot dog on wooden sticks. Dip in batter and fry in hot oil using sticks or tongs. Drain onto paper towels.

Pigs in the Blanket

head of cabbage

sausage, formed into small logs

Gently boil large leaves of cabbage to soften. Cool. Roll up the sausage logs inside the cabbage leaves and place into baking dish seam side down. Bake at 350°F for 35 minutes. Salt and pepper to taste. Meat loaf may also be used instead of sausage.

Chicken 'n' Broccoli Pie

1 pkg. frozen chopped broccoli

3 cups shredded cheddar cheese

1 ½ cups cut-up cooked chicken

2/3 cup chopped onion

1 ½ cups milk

3 eggs

¾ cup biscuit mix (see p. 93)

salt and pepper to taste

Preheat oven to 400°F. Grease 10" pie plate. Rinse broccoli under running cold water to thaw; drain thoroughly. Mix broccoli, 2 cups of cheese, chicken, and onion in plate. Beat milk, eggs, biscuit mix, salt, and pepper until smooth, about 1 minute by hand. Pour into plate. Bake until knife inserted in center comes out clean for about 25 to 35 minutes. Top with remaining cheese. Bake until cheese is melted for about 2 minutes. Cool for 5 minutes and serve.

Pizza Pie

1 1/3 cups chopped onion

1 /3 cup grated parmesan cheese

1 ½ cups milk

¾ cup biscuit mix (see p. 93)

2 cups shredded mozzarella cheese

3 ½ oz. sliced pepperoni

3 eggs

½ cup chopped green pepper

Preheat oven to 425°F. Make sauce and set aside (see below).
Grease 10" pie plate. Sprinkle 2/3 cup onion and parmesan cheese in plate. Beat eggs, milk, and biscuit mix until smooth about 1 minute by hand. Pour into plate. Bake for 20 minutes. Spread sauce over top. Layer meat, remaining onion, peppers, cheese on top of sauce. Bake until cheese is light brown, 15 to 20 minutes. Cool for 5 minutes and serve.

Pizza Sauce

6 oz. tomato paste   ¼ cup water

1 tsp. oregano leaves   ½ tsp. garlic salt

¼ tsp. pepper   ½ tsp. basil leaves

Mix tomato paste, water, oregano, garlic salt, basil, and pepper.

Onion Pie

1 to 1 ½ cup cracker crumbs, saltine, or soda

½ cup butter, melted

4 cups thinly sliced onions

4 eggs, slightly beaten

1 ½ cup milk

1 ½ tsp. salt

dash of pepper

1 cup shredded cheddar cheese

Preheat oven 350°F. Combine crumbs and ¼ cup melted butter and press against bottom and sides of pie plate. Sauté onions in ¼ cup melted butter until tender. Place cooked onions on pie crust. Mix eggs, milk, salt, and pepper and pour over onions. Sprinkle top of pie with shredded cheese. Bake 25 to 30 minutes or until set. Cool for 15 minutes before slicing. Variation: add diced ham. A family favorite!

Trout Almandine

6 trout fillets or other white fish   salt and pepper

1 cup milk   ½ lb. butter

½ cup flour   ¼ lb. sliced almonds

3 tbsp. lemon juice

Dip each fillet in the milk, and lightly dust with flour seasoned with salt and pepper. Melt the butter in a large skillet and brown the fillets on both sides. Remove the fish and keep warm. Add lemon juice and almonds to the skillet. Quickly bring the mixture to a boil. Stir constantly, scraping the bottom of the pan. When the almonds are golden, pour the mixture over the fillets and serve.

Fried Zucchini Patties

3 cups grated zucchini   1 egg
½ cup parmesan cheese   1 tsp. garlic salt
1 cup biscuit mix (see p. 93)

Mix all well and shape into patties. Let rest for 10 minutes. Fry in butter and serve.

Chicken Tortilla Casserole

12 corn or flour tortillas, torn into bite-size pieces
4 chicken breasts, cooked, deboned, skinless, chopped
1 lb. cheddar cheese

Sauce

1 cup milk   1 can cream of mushroom soup
1 can cream of chicken soup   green chili salsa
1 chopped onion, sautéed in butter

In a greased casserole dish, layer tortillas, chicken, sauce, cheese, salt, and pepper till all ingredients are in. Top with cheese. Cover and refrigerate overnight. The next day, bake at 350°F uncovered for 1 hour or until hot and bubbly. This is a large recipe. You can make two small casseroles and freeze the other for another day.

Progressive Dinner Potato Casserole

6 to 9 potatoes, cooked in jackets, peeled and diced
¼ cup butter
1 can cream of chicken (or mushroom) soup
1 pint sour cream
½ cup chopped green onion
1 ½ cup shredded cheese
2 tbsp. melted butter
crushed cornflakes

Melt ½ cup butter into skillet or saucepan until clear. Blend in soup, sour cream, onion, and cheese. Pour sauce over potatoes into casserole dish. Sprinkle with butter and cornflakes. Bake at 350°F for 45 minutes.

Barley Mushroom Stew

3 tbsp. olive oil   1 cup sliced mushrooms
1/8 tsp. pepper   ½ onion, minced
2 cups hot water   2 carrots, thinly sliced
½ cup pearl barley   2 beef bouillon cubes

Sauté onion, barley, and mushrooms in olive oil. Dissolve bouillon cubes in hot water and add barley mixture. Stir in pepper and carrots. Bring to a boil, reduce heat, and simmer for 25 minutes.

Hamburger Pie

1 cup biscuit baking mix (see p. 93)
¼ cup water
1 lb. lean ground beef
½ tsp. salt
½ tsp. oregano
¼ tsp. pepper

8 oz. tomato sauce

½ cup finely chopped bread crumbs

¼ cup chopped onion

¼ cup chopped green peppers

1 egg

¼ cup milk

½ tsp. salt

½ tsp. dry mustard

2 cups grated cheddar cheese

Heat oven to 375°F. Mix baking mix and water until soft dough forms. Beat vigorously in 20 strokes. Gently smooth dough into ball on top of floured cloth-covered board. Knead 5 times, and roll dough 2 inches larger than pie plate. Flute edges. Brown meat and drain. Stir in salt, oregano, pepper, bread crumbs, tomato sauce, onions, and green peppers. Spread in pie crust. Beat egg and milk; stir in remaining ingredients. Spread over beef mixture and bake until crust is golden for about 30 minutes.

Italian Barley Casserole

2 cups water	¾ cup milk
½ cup pearl barley	1 cup mozzarella cheese, grated
½ cup onion, diced	½ cup zucchini, diced
½ cup red pepper, diced	1 ½ tsp. flour
¼ tsp. salt	¼ tsp. pepper
1 tbsp. dry mustard	¼ tsp. basil
½ tsp. garlic powder	½ tsp. parsley, mined
¼ tsp. oregano	

Bring water to boil and add barley and salt. Cover and reduce heat and simmer for 45 minutes or until tender. Let stand covered for five minutes. Preheat oven to 375°F. Sauté onion, zucchini, and red pepper for 10 minutes or until tender. Stir in flour, salt, and pepper. Cook for 2 minutes. Add milk, stirring constantly until thick. Remove from heat. Add cooked barley, ¾ cup cheese, mustard, and spices. Stir until cheese melts. Spread in layers in 9"× 13" baking dish and top with cheese. Bake for 20 minutes or until hot. Broil until cheese is lightly brown.

Pinwheels

Make biscuits (p.11) and roll out to one-inch thick. Make meat loaf (p. 25) and put on top of rolled-out biscuits. Roll up together and pinch ends. Cut into one-inch slices and bake on greased cookie sheet for 20 to 25 minutes at 350°F. Cover with gravy (pp. 11, 25) Extra pinwheels freeze well.

Granny's Scalloped Potatoes

3 tbsp. butter	2 tbsp. flour
3 cups milk	1 tsp. salt
¼ tsp. pepper	6 medium potatoes, sliced thinly
2 tbsp. chopped onions	chopped ham
cheese, grated	

Put half of the potatoes in baking dish. Sprinkle with half of the flour, salt and pepper, dot with butter. Repeat with layer; add milk until it is half way up the dish, add chopped ham; top with cheese. Cover, bake for 1 hour at 350°F. Uncover and brown. Serves 4 to 6

Twice-Baked Potatoes

baking potatoes	bacon, cooked, chopped
green onions, chopped	milk
butter	salt and pepper
Edam cheese, grated	

Bake potatoes at 400°F for 1 hour. Remove from oven; slice potatoes in halves. Scoop out potatoes into a bowl; stir in bacon, green onions, butter, milk, and spices to taste. Put back in potato skins and top with Edam cheese; bake for an additional 10 minutes or until cheese is melted and browned.

Creamed Vegetables with Bacon

1 tbsp. butter

dash of salt and pepper to taste

2 cups canned vegetables

1 tbsp. flour

¾ cup milk

1 cup chopped bacon

Make white sauce of butter, flour, spices, and milk. Cook and drain veggies; put into baking dish. Top with white sauce, heat, and serve.

Potato Mushroom Bake

3 medium potatoes, sliced with skins

¼ lb. fresh mushrooms, sliced

1 tsp. tarragon leaves

2 tbsp. parsley

1 medium onion, sliced

¾ tsp. salt and pepper to taste

1 cup heavy cream

In a buttered baking dish, layer potatoes, onion, and mushrooms. Sprinkle salt, pepper, and tarragon. Pour in cream. Cover with foil and bake at 350°F for 30 minutes or until potatoes are fork tender and sauce has thickened. Sprinkle with parsley and serve. Dish can be made ahead and baked right before dinner. May be topped with cheese before baking.

Veggie and Ham Casserole

1 can green beans

½ cup chopped onion

2 tbsp. butter

1 can stewed tomatoes

½ tsp. seasoning salt

1 cup chopped ham

In a saucepan, melt butter, sauté onions and ham, add green beans and stewed tomatoes, and simmer for 30 minutes. Add seasoning salt and serve. Bacon may be substituted for ham.

Double Cheese Linguine

1 pkg. linguine, cooked	2 tbsp. butter
3 tbsp. flour	salt and pepper to taste
1 ½ cup milk	2 tbsp. lemon juice
¾ cup mozzarella cheese, grated	¼ cup parmesan cheese, grated

Cook linguine according to directions. In a skillet, melt butter. Stir in flour, salt, and pepper until smooth. Gradually, stir in milk. Bring to boil and stir for 2 minutes or until thickened. Remove from heat. Combine cheeses and toss with lemon juice. Add cheese sauce; stir until noodles are well coated.

Sliced Tomato Pie

Cornmeal Pie Shell (see below)	6 to 8 medium tomatoes
¼ cup mayonnaise	¼ cup plain yogurt
1 garlic button, chopped	¼ tsp. salt and pepper to taste
2 tbsp. butter	½ cup chopped parsley
½ cup chopped green onions	½ cup soft bread crumbs
¼ cup grated parmesan cheese	

Prepare pie shell and partially bake as directed. Slice tomatoes and layer in pie shell. Combine mayonnaise, yogurt, and garlic and spread over tomatoes. Season with salt and pepper. Melt butter and sauté green onions for a few minutes. Stir in bread crumbs, parsley, and cheese. Sprinkle over tomatoes. Bake at 350°F for 30 minutes. Let sit for 10 minutes before cutting.

Cornmeal Pie Shell

¾ cup plus 2 tbsp. flour	2 tbsp. yellow cornmeal
2 tbsp. water	6 tbsp. butter

Combine flour and yellow cornmeal. Remove 2 heaping tbsp. and combine with water to make a paste. Cut in 6 tbsp. butter and remaining flour. Roll out and put into pie pan. Partially bake at 450°F for 5 minutes.

Mushroom Penne Pasta

1 pkg. penne pasta	1 cup mushrooms
2 tbsp. olive oil	2 tbsp. parsley, chopped
2 cloves garlic, chopped	salt and pepper

Cook penne pasta according to package directions. Drain and set aside. In a skillet, sauté garlic, mushrooms, and parsley in olive oil. Add pasta, stirring to coat and serve.

Broccoli Ricotta Lasagna

12 lasagna noodles, cooked and drained	16 oz. ricotta cheese
3 eggs, beaten	1 tsp. basil
2 tbsp. butter	½ cup onion, chopped
2 cloves garlic, chopped	¼ cup flour
2 cups milk	1 cup mozzarella cheese, grated
1 small tomato, chopped	2 tbsp. parmesan cheese

Cook lasagna noodles according to package directions. Set aside. In bowl, combine ricotta cheese, eggs, and basil. Set aside. Preheat oven to 350°F. In a skillet, sauté onion and garlic in butter. Stir in flour. Cook for 1 minute. Gradually stir in milk. Cook, stirring until sauce thickens and begins to boil. Remove from heat and stir in broccoli and cheese. Place 1/3 of the noodles in baking dish. Top with 1/3 ricotta-egg mixture and 1/3 broccoli-cheese mixture. Repeat layers 2 more times. Top with chopped tomatoes and parmesan cheese. Bake for 1 hour or until set. Let stand for 10 minutes before serving.

Eggplant Zucchini Bake

1 tsp. olive oil	1 tbsp. butter
½ cup onion, chopped	2 cloves garlic, minced
1 large can whole tomatoes	1 tbsp. tomato paste
2 tsp. basil	1 tsp. oregano
2 cups zucchini, sliced	2 medium eggplants, peeled and chopped
1 cup mushrooms, sliced	parmesan cheese

Preheat oven to 350°F. Heat oil and butter in a skillet; sauté onion and garlic. Add tomatoes, tomato paste, basil, and oregano. Cook until sauce thickens for about 5 minutes. Place eggplant, zucchini, and mushrooms in 9" baking dish. Pour sauce over eggplant mixture. Cover and bake for 30 minutes. Top with cheese.

Little Italy Stuffed Tomatoes

2 large ripe tomatoes	1 cup instant rice, cooked
1 tsp. basil	1 tsp. oregano
½ tsp. salt	¼ tsp. garlic powder
1 tbsp. olive oil	¼ cup parmesan cheese, grated
2 tbsp. bread crumbs	1 tbsp. parsley, chopped

Preheat oven to 200°F. Cut tomatoes in half. Spoon out the inside pulp and seeds, leaving 4 tomato cups. Mix pulp and rice, basil, oregano, salt, and garlic powder. Spoon ¼ mixture into each tomato cups. Combine olive oil, parmesan cheese, bread crumbs, and parsley. Top each tomato cup. Place in baking dish and bake for 10 minutes or until heated through. Broil 2 minutes until topping is browned.

Veggie Chili

1 tbsp. olive oil

½ cup red onion, chopped

½ cup red pepper, chopped

2 tbsp. chili powder

1 large can whole tomatoes

2 cloves garlic, minced

2 cups mushrooms, sliced

¼ tsp. cumin

¼ tsp. oregano

1 cup chili beans, cooked

Sauté garlic in oil. Add mushrooms, onion, and pepper. Cook for 5 minutes. Add spices. Add tomatoes and beans. Reduce heat and simmer for 30 minutes, stirring occasionally.

Zucchini Mushroom Frittata

1 tbsp. olive oil

1 medium tomato, chopped

6 eggs, beaten

½ cup swiss cheese, grated

salt and pepper

1 medium zucchini, grated

1 can mushrooms, drained

¼ cup milk

½ tsp. garlic powder

In a skillet, sauté zucchini, tomatoes, and mushrooms in olive oil until tender. In bowl, mix eggs, cheese, milk, garlic powder, salt, and pepper. Pour into skillet, stirring well. Cover and simmer 15 minutes. Remove lid and broil for 3 minutes.

Granny's Favorite
International Recipes

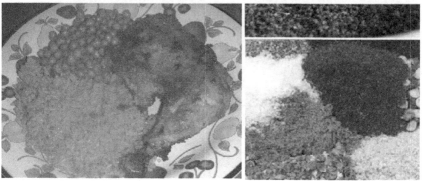

Spanish Rice... page 45   *Taco Seasoning... page 45*

Sopaipillas Mexican Fried Cookie... page 48

Taco Dip

1 lb. lean ground beef	1 dry pkg. taco seasoning
6 oz. green taco sauce	16 oz. can refried beans
16 oz. sour cream	1 cup shredded cheddar cheese

Brown meat. Add taco seasoning, taco sauce, and refried beans. Mix well. Pour into loaf pan; spoon sour cream over and top with cheese. Bake at 350°F for 30 minutes. Eat with nacho chips.

Taco Seasoning

2 tsp. chili powder

1 ½ tsp. ground cumin

¾ tsp. garlic salt

dash of cayenne pepper

1 ½ tsp. paprika

1 tsp. onion powder

½ tsp. salt

Combine all ingredients. Makes 3 tbsp. seasoning.

Jalapeño Bean Dip

5 small jalapeño peppers

1 tbsp. oil

½ tsp. oregano

2 ½ cups chili hot beans, mashed

½ tsp. salt

¼ tsp. garlic powder

Cut off tops of peppers. Combine whole peppers and remaining ingredients in a saucepan. Simmer for 15 minutes; add water if needed to keep beans from sticking. Cool mixture and remove peppers. Serve dip with fresh veggies or crackers.

Spanish Rice

1 cup uncooked rice

2/3 cup chopped onion and green peppers

2 tbsp. olive oil

1 cup water

½ tsp. mustard

1 tsp. salt

¼ tsp. pepper

1 beef bouillon cube

2 cups chopped canned tomatoes

1 tsp. worcestershire sauce

Sauté rice, onion, and peppers in oil until veggies are tender. Add remaining ingredients. Bring to a boil. Reduce heat and simmer for 20 minutes or until liquid is absorbed and rice is tender. Serves 6 to 8.

Burroladas

Sauce

24 oz. tomato sauce	1 can tomato soup
16 oz. can chopped tomatoes	1 ½ cups water
1 tsp. chili powder	1 tsp. garlic powder
1 tsp. ground cumin	1 tsp. oregano
1 tsp. salt	

Blend all ingredients in a saucepan over medium heat. Stir and bring to a boil. Reduce to simmer; cover and continue for 5 to 10 minutes. Set aside.

Filling

2 tbsp. oil	lean ground beef
8 oz. sliced mushrooms, drained	1 cup finely chopped onion
3 cups grated Jack cheese	12 flour tortillas

Heat oil in frying pan. Add meat, onions, and mushrooms and brown. Add 1 ½ cups of sauce to meat; stir and simmer for 10 minutes. Remove from heat. Grease two 9"× 13" baking dishes. Spread ½ cup meat mixture on each tortilla and sprinkle 2 tbsp. grated cheese. Preheat oven to 350°F. Roll up and place seam down into greased pans. Place 6 in each pan with ½ inch between each burrolada. Divide remainder of sauce, and pour each half evenly over each pan. Cover and bake in for 20 minutes. Remove cover and sprinkle remaining cheese and bake uncovered for 10 minutes or until bubbly. Let stand for at least 5 minutes before serving. Serves 12.

Rip Snortin' Chili

1 can chili beans	2 cans Italian stewed tomatoes, chopped
1 can Nacho Cheese soup	½ cup Cheez Whiz
1 lb. lean ground beef	1 lb. Italian sausage
1 medium onion, chopped	1 can mushrooms
1 can tomato sauce	nacho chips
shredded cheddar cheese	

Brown meat, onion, mushrooms; drain grease off. Put in Crock-Pot with rest of the ingredients except chips and cheese and slow cook for 2 hours. Top with crushed nacho chips and shredded cheddar cheese.

Mexican Hot Dish

1 lb. pork sausage	¼ cup chopped onion
½ cup chopped green peppers	1 cup uncooked macaroni
2 tbsp. sugar	1 tsp. salt
1 tsp. chili powder	1 lb. can tomatoes
½ cup sour cream	grated cheese

Brown meat and drain off fat. Add onions and green peppers. Cook until tender. Stir in rest of ingredients except sour cream and grated cheese. Cover and simmer for 20 minutes. Check macaroni to make sure it is cooked tender. Stir in sour cream and heat. Add grated cheese on each serving.

Mexican Chicken

3 cups cooked chicken, cubed
2 cans cream of mushroom soup
16 oz. can tomatoes and green chili sauce
Doritos chips
shredded cheddar cheese

Mix chicken, soup, chili sauce. In large greased baking dish, layer bottom with Doritos chips. Add ½ chicken mix; sprinkle with half the cheese. Repeat layers with Doritos on top. Bake at 350°F for 30 minutes until bubbly.

Taco Pizza

1 lb. lean ground beef	1 pkg. taco seasoning
1 pkg. flour tortillas	16 oz. refried beans
2 medium chopped onions	16 oz. sour cream
1 lb. grated cheddar cheese	3 medium chopped tomatoes
¼ head lettuce, chopped	

Preheat oven to 350°F. Brown and drain meat; add taco mix and ¾ cup water. Simmer for 10 minutes. Heat refried beans according to instructions on can and set aside. On a cookie sheet, spread flour tortillas to cover pan. Spread refried beans over tortillas. Add seasoned meat and top with onions. Next add grated cheese. Bake until cheese is melted, for approximately 10 minutes. Remove from oven and add tomatoes and finally lettuce. Bake for an additional 5 minutes and remove from oven. Cut into squares. Serve with sour cream.

Sopaipillas Mexican Fried Cookie

4 cups flour	2 tsp. baking powder
2 tsp. salt	2 tsp. shortening
1 ¼ cups water	

Sift together flour, baking powder, and salt. Add shortening, water, and knead until smooth. Put into plastic bag and let stand for 2 hours. Roll very thick and cut into triangles. Fry in deep fat heated to 375°F until golden brown. Turn once. Drain on paper towels and serve with honey or sprinkled with cinnamon sugar. Serves 12.

Fettuccine Alfredo

8 oz. medium egg noodles

½ cup heavy cream

½ cup butter

1 cup parmesan cheese

pepper to taste

Grate cheese. Cut butter into quarters. Cook noodles, drain. In a saucepan, combine cheese, butter, and cream. Cook over medium heat for 3 to 4 minutes or until butter melts. Stir in drained noodles, toss well. Season and serve. Serves 4.

Italian Bread

1 tbsp. sugar

2 pkgs. active dry yeast

5 cups flour

water

1 egg white

2 tsp. salt

cornmeal

1 tbsp. butter

salad oil

In large bowl, combine sugar, salt, yeast, and 2 cups flour. In a small saucepan over low heat, put butter and 1 ¾ cups water until very warm (butter does not need to melt). With mixer at low speed, gradually beat liquid into dry ingredients until just blended. Beat for 2 minutes on medium speed. Beat in ½ cup flour to make thick batter for 2 more minutes. Scrape bowl often with spatula. With wooden spoon, stir in enough additional flour (about 1 ¾ cups) to make a soft dough. Turn dough onto floured surface; knead until smooth and elastic, for about 10 minutes, adding flour while kneading. Cut dough in half; cover pieces with bowl. Let dough rest for 20 minutes for easier shaping.

Grease large cookie sheet, sprinkle with cornmeal. On floured surface with floured rolling pin, roll each half into 15"× 10" rectangle. From 15" side, tightly roll dough; pinch seam to seal. Place loaves, seam side down, on cookie sheet and taper ends. Brush loaves with oil; cover loosely with plastic wrap. Refrigerate for 2 to 24 hours. Preheat oven to 425°F. Remove loaves from fridge, uncover. Let stand for 10 minutes. Cut slashes on top of each loaf and bake for 20 minutes. Brush with beaten egg white, and bake for 5 more minutes.

Granny's Favorite
Salad Recipes

Cabbage Salsa... page 51

Potato Salad... page 59

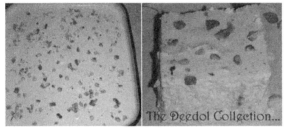

Lemon Lime Jell-O Salad... page 52

Spinach Salad... page 60

Cabbage Salsa

½ head of cabbage	2 Roma tomatoes	2 limes
½ bunch cilantro	¼ red onion	¼ white onion
3 canned jalapeños	oregano	salt and pepper

Chop all veggies and add lime juice. Mix well and spice to taste.

Lemon Lime Jell-O Salad

3 oz. lemon flavor gelatin
1 cup heavy whipped cream
3 oz. lime flavor gelatin
1 cup crushed pineapple

2 cups boiling water
1 ½ cup cottage cheese
1 cup pineapple juice
1 cup walnuts

Dissolve lemon gelatin in 1 cup boiling water and chill until slightly thickened. Beat until light and fluffy. Next fold in whipped cream, add cottage cheese, and mix well. Pour into Jell-O molds, ½ full only. Dissolve lime gelatin in 1 cup boiling water and add pineapple juice. Chill until slightly thickened. Add pineapple and pour on top of lemon Jell-O. Fill to top.

Tangy Tomato Aspic

1 ¼ cup boiling water
8 oz. tomato sauce
½ tsp. salt
¼ tsp. red pepper sauce
2 cups diced celery
small can shrimp

3 oz. lemon flavor gelatin
1 ½ tbsp. vinegar
½ tsp. onion juice or grated onions
dash of cloves
mayonnaise or salad dressing

Dissolve gelatin in boiling water. Stir in tomato sauce, vinegar, and seasonings. Chill until slightly thickened but not set. Stir in celery. Pour into 4 cup molds or into 6 individual molds. Chill until firm. If desired, garnish with ripe olives. Serve with mayonnaise or salad dressing and top with shrimp.

Broccoli Salad

1 bunch broccoli, chopped finely
2 tomatoes, chopped
1 pkg. Good Seasons Italian dressing mix

12 fresh mushrooms, chopped
1 ripe avocado, chopped
1 cup mayonnaise

Chop and toss broccoli, mushrooms, tomatoes, and avocado and set aside. Mix dressing with Italian mix and mayonnaise. Mix with veggies and serve.

Curried Spinach Salad

1 lb. fresh spinach	¼ tsp. curry powder
2 tbsp. lemon juice	4 scallions, finely sliced
2 tbsp. olive oil	½ cup chopped salted pecans or walnuts

Wash spinach and remove coarse stems. Tear into bite-sized pieces and pat dry with paper towel.

Dressing

In jar with lid, combine lemon juice, olive oil, and curry powder. Shake until thoroughly combined. Put spinach in a salad bowl and toss to mix with salad dressing. Top with salted nuts. Serves 4 to 6.

Fruit Emerald Salad

3 oz. pkg. lemon gelatin	3 oz. pkg. lime gelatin
1 ½ cups pineapple juice	1 cup crushed pineapple
1 cup mayonnaise	1 cup cottage cheese
1 cup canned milk	1 cup any fresh fruit, drained

Heat pineapple juice and dissolve gelatin in it. Chill until partially set and fold in remaining ingredients. Chill until firm and serve.

Avocado Salad

1 head iceberg lettuce	1 head red leaf lettuce
1 ripe avocado	small red onion
½ cup balsamic vinegar	

Wash, dry, and tear the lettuce into bite-size pieces. Toss with diced avocado and sliced onions. Dress with balsamic vinegar and serve.

Marinated Tomato Salad

1 ½ cup white wine vinegar
¼ cup shallots, chopped
2 tbsp. lemon juice
2 tbsp. extra virgin olive oil
2 large yellow tomatoes, sliced
16 yellow pear tomatoes, halved

½ tsp. salt
2 tbsp. chives, chopped
white pepper
6 plum tomatoes, quartered vertically
16 red cherry tomatoes, halved

Combine vinegar and salt in large bowl. Stir until salt is dissolved. Add shallots, chives, lemon juice, and white pepper and mix well. Slowly whisk in oil until well blended. Add tomatoes and toss well. Cover and let stand at room temperature for 2 to 3 hours.

Tortellini Salad

9 oz. tortellini or ravioli noodles, cooked
1 cup sliced carrots
tomato, chopped

3 cups broccoli florets
¼ cups sliced green onions
ranch dressing

Cook pasta according to package directions. Add the broccoli and carrots during the last 3 minutes of cooking. Drain and rinse with cold water; drain again. In large bowl, combine cooked pasta mixture and green onions. Drizzle with dressing and gently toss to coat. Cover and chill for 24 hours (minimum of 2 hours). Just before serving, stir in tomato. If too thick, thin with a little milk.

Tomato Salad

1 bottle oil and vinegar salad dressing
1 cup water
black pepper
1 pint cherry tomatoes

3 tbsp. apple cider vinegar
salt
1 pint pear tomatoes
3 golden harvest tomatoes, sliced

3 Roma tomatoes, sliced   1 bell pepper, sliced
1 sweet onion, sliced

Whisk together the oil and vinegar dressing, apple cider vinegar, and water. Add the tomatoes, peppers, and onion and toss well to coat. Add salt and pepper to taste. DO NOT refrigerate for best flavor.

Chicken Salad

1/3 cup cooked chicken or turkey, chopped
taco shells
2 tbsp. celery, chopped
1 tbsp. dressing
1 tbsp. salsa
1 tbsp. cheddar cheese, grated

In bowl, combine chicken, celery, dressing, and cheese and toss well. Fill taco shells with salad mixture.

Chinese Slaw Salad

16 oz. coleslaw cabbage mix   5 green onions, chopped
sliced almonds   cooked chicken, diced
2 pkgs. chicken ramen noodles, broken into small pieces
½ cup sugar   1/4 cup oil
1/3 cup apple cider vinegar   2 pkgs. chicken
ramen seasoning mix   sunflower seeds

Mix slaw mix with green onions, chicken, almonds, and broken ramen noodles and set aside. Mix together sugar, oil, apple cider vinegar, and chicken ramen seasoning. Add to slaw mixture and chill for 2 hours. Top with sunflower seeds.

Variations: Shred 4 cups cabbage and 1 carrot and use in place of coleslaw cabbage mix. Use rice vinegar in place of apple cider vinegar.

Brain Power Salad

¼ cup mayonnaise

1 tsp. cider vinegar

½ cup carrots, shredded

¼ cup water chestnuts, drained

2 tbsp. crumbled bacon, cooked

2 tsp. sugar

2 cups broccoli florets

¼ cup cheddar cheese, shredded

2 tbsp. red onion, chopped

For dressing, stir together mayo, sugar, vinegar. Combine veggies and cheese. Pour dressing over salad and serve.

BLT Salad

5 cups baby spinach leaves

2 cups grape or cherry tomatoes, halved

½ lb. bacon, cooked crispy, drained, and crumbled

2 hard-boiled eggs, chopped

1/3 cup ranch salad dressing

Place spinach in bowl. Top with tomatoes, bacon, and chopped egg. Drizzle with dressing and toss well.

Fruit Salad

1 can fruit cocktail, drained

2 bananas, sliced

½ cup whipped cream

1 cup crushed pineapple, drained

1 can mandarin oranges, drained

Mix fruit and fold in whipped cream.

Waldorf Salad

1 cup apples, diced	1 tsp. lemon juice
1 cup celery, diced	½ cup raisins
½ cup nuts, chopped	½ cup mayonnaise
2 tbsp. milk	1 tsp. sugar

Toss apples with lemon juice until well coated. Add celery, raisins, and nuts. Toss well. In bowl, stir mayo and milk to thin it. Stir in sugar until well blended. Toss salad with dressing until well coated. Chill and serve.

Summer Salad

2 cups watermelon, cubed	1 cup blueberries
grated coconut	1 cup cantaloupe, cubed
1 cup seedless green grapes	

Combine, chill, and serve.

Fruit Delight

10 oz. whipped topping	1 can fruit cocktail, drained
6 oz. cherry gelatin	1 pint small curd cottage cheese, drained

Combine, chill, and serve.

Spinach Parmesan Salad

1 bunch spinach leaves, torn	1 small red onion, minced
3 slices bacon, cook and crumbled	2 tbsp. olive oil
2 tbsp. parmesan cheese, grated	1 tbsp. parsley, minced

Combine spinach, onion, bacon, and fresh parmesan. Mix oil, parmesan, and parsley and drizzle over salad and toss.

Three-Bean Salad

1 can cut green beans

1 can kidney beans

1 small onion

1 tsp. vinegar

pepper to taste

1 can yellow beans

1 small green pepper

½ cup sugar

1 tsp. salt

1/3 cup olive oil

Drain beans; dice peppers and onions. Combine all until well mixed. Chill and serve.

Sour Cream Fruit Salad

1 cup sour cream

1 cup shredded coconut

1 cup mini marshmallows

2 cups any fresh fruit, cubed

Mix well, chill, and serve.

Shrimp Salad

¾ cup macaroni, cooked

1 cup black olives, sliced

2 eggs, hard boiled and sliced

2 tbsp. vinegar

½ cup cheddar cheese, grated

2 cups cabbage, shredded

½ cup mayonnaise

2 tsp. mustard

1 cup shrimp

Chill cooked macaroni until cold. Add olives, eggs, shrimp, and cabbage. Toss lightly. In a small bowl, combine mayo, mustard, vinegar, salt, and pepper to taste. Mix well and stir into salad until well coated.

Seven-Layer Salad

1 head lettuce, chopped	2 stalks celery, chopped
1 sweet onion, chopped	1 green pepper, chopped
10 oz. pkg. frozen peas, thawed	1 cucumber, chopped
2 cups mayonnaise	2 tbsp. sugar
1 cup parmesan cheese, grated	½ cup bacon, cooked and crumbled

Layer lettuce, celery, onion, green pepper, cucumber, and peas in large bowl. Spread mayo over top to the edges of the bowl and sprinkle sugar, cheese, and bacon. Refrigerate until served.

Coleslaw

½ head cabbage, shredded	1 carrot, grated
½ onion, chopped	½ cup mayonnaise
2 tbsp. lemon juice	salt and pepper

Combine cabbage, carrot, and onion and set aside. In small bowl, stir together mayo, lemon juice, salt, and pepper. Add dressing to cabbage mixture. Chill and serve.

Potato Salad

5 lbs. potatoes, cooked and cubed	2 cups celery, chopped
1 sweet onion, chopped	6 dill pickles, chopped
8 eggs, hard boiled	1 cup mayonnaise
2 tbsp. mustard	salt and pepper
paprika	

Mix potatoes, celery, onion, pickles, and 6 chopped hard-boiled eggs together in large bowl. In small bowl, add mayo, mustard, salt, and pepper. Add to salad mixture and mix well. Slice up last 2 eggs and lay on top of salad. Sprinkle paprika over top. Chill and serve.

Spinach Salad

baby spinach leaves   1 can black olives, sliced
fresh mushrooms   real bacon bits
1 can water chestnuts   feta cheese
croutons   sunflower seeds
oil and vinegar or balsamic vinaigrette

Put water chestnuts in 1 cup dressing overnight. Next day, toss salad with crumbled feta cheese, topping with croutons. Pour on dressing over salad.

Hot Dutch Potato Salad

2 slices bacon   ½ cup onion, chopped
3 tbsp. cider vinegar   1 tbsp. water
2 tbsp. sugar   ½ tsp. salt
dash of pepper   2 potatoes, cooked and diced

Dice bacon into fine pieces and fry until crispy and brown. Add onion and cook until browned. Add vinegar, water, sugar, salt, and pepper. Bring to a boil. Add potatoes. Heat through. Serve hot.

Taco Salad

1 lb. lean ground beef   taco seasoning
1 head lettuce, torn   1 medium onion, chopped
4 diced tomatoes   black olives, sliced
1 can kidney beans, drained   2 cups cheddar cheese, grated
hot sauce, to taste   sour cream
¼ tsp. salt   guacamole sauce
corn chips, crushed

Brown meat in taco seasoning according to package directions and cool. Tear lettuce and top with onion, tomatoes, beans, olives, and cheese. Top with meat and corn chips. Mix sour cream, guacamole, salt, and hot sauce for dressing.

Raspberry Cooler

1 cup applesauce

3 oz. pkg. raspberry gelatin

1 cup raspberries

1 cup nuts, chopped

Heat applesauce until it boils. Dissolve gelatin in it and stir in raspberries. Fold in nuts. Chill until firm.

Guacamole

1 ripe avocado, mashed

1 tsp. salt

¼ tsp. chili or cayenne pepper

¼ tsp. cumin

¼ cup sour cream

1 tsp. lemon juice

½ cup onion, diced

¼ tsp. garlic

2 tsp. cilantro, chopped

1 tomato, chopped

Combine all and store covered in refrigerator until serving.

French Dressing

¾ cup salad oil

1 tbsp. sugar

¼ tsp. paprika

¼ tsp. onion salt

¼ cup lemon juice or vinegar

¾ tsp. salt

¼ tsp. dry mustard

¼ tsp. pepper

Mix all well. Store in refrigerator until ready to use.

Green Salad Dressing

1 cup mayonnaise
1 tsp. lemon juice
garlic powder
celery salt
pepper

1 cup milk
2 eggs, hard boiled and minced
onion salt
parsley

Mix all well and spice to taste.

Roquefort Dressing

2 oz. Roquefort cheese
½ cup buttermilk

½ cup mayonnaise
salt and pepper to taste

Mash cheese with fork. Beat in buttermilk and mayo until smooth. Add spices to taste.

Italian Dressing

1 cup olive oil
1 tsp. sugar
½ tsp. celery salt
¼ tsp. red pepper

½ cup vinegar
½ tsp. salt
¼ tsp. dry mustard
¼ tsp. garlic powder

Mix all well and refrigerate until needed.

Thousand Island Dressing

1 cup mayonnaise

2 tbsp. sweet pickle relish

1 tbsp. onion, minced

1 hard-boiled egg, chopped

2 tbsp. ketchup

1 tbsp. green pepper, minced

½ tsp. salt

dash of pepper

Mix all and refrigerate until needed.

Catalina Dressing

½ cup sugar

1/3 cup vinegar

salt and pepper to taste

2/3 cup olive oil

1/3 cup catsup

1 small onion, grated

Blend all ingredients well. Makes almost 2 cups of dressing.

Quick Dressing

1 cup mayonnaise

1 tbsp. dill pickle juice

½ cup ketchup

½ tbsp. worcestershire sauce

Mix all well and keep refrigerated until ready to use.

Quick Ranch Dressing

1 cup Miracle Whip salad dressing

1 tsp. salt

½ tsp. garlic powder

2 tsp. parsley

1 cup buttermilk

½ tsp. pepper

½ tsp. onion powder

Mix all well and store in fridge.

Caesar Salad Dressing

¼ cup olive oil

½ cup parmesan cheese

1 clove garlic

pinch of sugar

¼ cup wine vinegar

4 anchovies

1 egg

Mix all well and refrigerate until ready to use.

Ranch Dressing Mix

¼ cup powdered buttermilk

1 tsp. salt

1 tbsp. dried minced chives

½ tsp. ground celery seed

3 tbsp. dried minced onion

3 tbsp. dried minced parsley

½ tsp. garlic powder

½ tsp. pepper

Put all in bowl and mix well. Store in jar with airtight lid until ready to use. Makes 8 cups of dressing.

To mix dressing: combine 1 ½ tbsp. ranch mix to ½ cup milk and ½ cup mayonnaise.

Western Dressing

¼ cup catsup

¼ cup cider vinegar

¼ tsp. garlic salt

¼ cup olive oil

6 tbsp. sugar

¼ tsp. celery salt

Mix well and refrigerate until used. Makes 1 cup.

Shake and Toss Dressing

1 clove garlic	1 ¼ tsp. salt
1/3 cup olive oil	½ bell pepper minced
3 tbsp. red onion minced	1 carrot, peeled and grated
2 tbsp. water	3 tbsp. white wine vinegar
2 tbsp. minced fresh parsley	pepper

Smash the garlic clove, sprinkle with salt, and with the flat side of a large knife, mash and smear the mixture to a coarse paste. Shake the garlic paste, oil, onion, bell pepper, carrot, vinegar, parsley, water, and pepper in a cruet. Serve. Refrigerate until used.

Avocado Dressing

1 large avocado, peeled and mashed with 2 tbsp. lemon juice
1 cup mayonnaise
½ cup sour cream
½ tsp. worcestershire sauce
1/3 cup chopped onion
2 cloves garlic, minced
1 tsp. salt
dash of cayenne pepper

Place all into food processor and blend until smooth. Chill and serve.

Red Wine Vinaigrette

½ cup red wine vinegar	3 tbsp. lemon juice
2 tsp. honey	2 tsp. salt
fresh ground black pepper	1 cup olive oil

Mix the vinegar, lemon juice, honey, salt, and pepper. Gradually blend in oil while stirring the dressing constantly. Chill and serve.

Basic Vinaigrette

¼ cup white wine vinegar   2 tsp. dijon mustard
1 tsp. salt pepper to taste   2/3 cup extra virgin olive oil

Whisk together the vinegar, mustard, salt, and pepper. Gradually whisk in oil, enough to make a smooth dressing with a balanced taste. Chill and refrigerate until used.

Herb Oil

½ bunch parsley   ½ cup packed fresh basil
½ bunch fresh thyme   ½ cup packed fresh oregano
½ orange, zested   1 dried arbol chili
1 tsp. whole black peppercorns   2 cups canola oil
1 cup olive oil

In a mason jar, place all the herbs, zest, chili, and peppercorns. Pour both oils into a saucepan and heat to 200°F. Pour the hot oils into the jar and cover with towel. Let stand overnight. Place cheesecloth over the top of the jar; add a ring to the jar. Strain oil into desired container. Refrigerate until used.

Blue Cheese Dressing

12 oz. sour cream   12 oz. mayonnaise
6 oz. crumbled blue cheese   3 oz. heavy cream
½ oz. worcestershire sauce   salt and pepper
garlic powder to taste   splash of lemon juice

Mix all well and refrigerate until ready to use.

Granny's Favorite
Side Dish Recipes

Perfect Rice... page 71

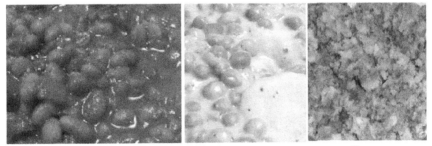

Baked Beans... page 75   *Creamed Potatoes and Peas... page 69*   *Stove Top Stuffing... page 76*

Green Bean Casserole

2 cans French-style green bean, drained

1 cup sour cream

1 can french fried onion rings

1 can cream of mushroom soup

Preheat oven to 325°F. Stir beans, sour cream, and soup together. Top with onion rings and bake for 20 minutes or until bubbly hot.

Cabbage Stew

1 head of red cabbage, torn

1 onion, sliced

3 large tomatoes, sliced

1 link polish sausage, sliced

1 lb. red potatoes

1 bell pepper sliced

Water to cover. Stew all until all is tender. Serve with corn bread or muffins.

Golden Onion Rings

½ cup flour

½ tsp. baking powder

¼ tsp. salt

1 egg, beaten

½ cup milk

1 tbsp. cooking oil

2 onions, sliced and separated

cooking oil for frying

Blend flour, baking powder, and salt. Beat together egg, milk, and oil. Stir into flour mixture until well blended. Dip onions into batter and drop into hot oil heated at 350°F, turning over when golden brown. Remove from oil onto paper towel to drain. Serve

French Fries

5 potatoes, peeled and cut into strips

1 ½ tsp. salt

hot oil or butter for frying

dash of pepper

Heat oil in deep fryer or butter in a skillet. Drop prepared potatoes into fat and fry until crispy golden brown. Remove to paper towel to drain. Season with salt and pepper.

Creamed Potatoes and Peas

2 lbs. red potatoes, boiled

3 tbsp. flour

¼ tsp. pepper

1 cup evaporated milk

½ cup onion, diced

¼ cup butter

1 ½ tsp. salt

1 ½ cups milk

10 oz. frozen peas

4 slices bacon, cooked and crumbled

Preheat oven to 325°F. Cut potatoes in half and place on greased baking pan. Sprinkle peas over potatoes. In a saucepan, melt butter and stir in flour, salt, and pepper. Add milk, stirring constantly until of right consistency. Pour sauce over vegetables. Top with bacon and bake for 20 to 25 minutes.

Texas Spuds

1 potatoes boiled and sliced

2 tbsp. flour

½ tsp. salt

½ cup onion, diced

¼ cup BBQ sauce (see pp. 213-214)

1 cup cheddar cheese, shredded

¼ cup butter

1 cup milk

¼ tsp. pepper

¼ cup green pepper, diced

Preheat oven to 350°F. Place half of potatoes in 8"× 8" baking dish. In a saucepan, melt butter and stir in flour. Add milk gradually, stirring constantly until of right consistency. Remove from heat. Stir in salt, pepper, onions, green peppers, and BBQ sauce. Stir in cheese until melted and pour over half of potatoes. Place last half of potatoes in baking dish and cover with remainder of sauce. Bake for 25 minutes or until bubbly and golden brown.

Skillet Scalloped Potatoes

2 potatoes, peeled and thinly sliced

2 tbsp. olive oil

¼ tsp. salt

dash of pepper
1 can evaporated milk
2 slices bacon, cooked and crumbled
½ cup cheese, grated

Brown potatoes in frying pan with small amount of oil. When tender, sprinkle with salt and pepper. Add milk, bacon, and cheese. Cover and simmer over low heat for 10 minutes or until sauce thickens.

Seasoned Potato Slices

2 potatoes, thinly sliced with skins on   garlic powder
onion salt   olive oil
pepper to taste

Lay potatoes in greased baking pan. Brush tops with olive oil, and sprinkle with spices. Place under broiler until browned. Remove from oven, and turn over to broil other side.

Zesty Zucchini

2 zucchini, peeled and cubed   2 eggs, beaten
¼ cup milk   1 tsp. baking powder
2 tbsp. flour   ½ lb. cheese, cubed
¼ cup onion, chopped   ¼ cup green pepper, chopped
garlic powder

Preheat oven at 350°F. Boil zucchini for 5 minutes just before tender. Drain and let cool. Combine eggs, milk, baking powder, cheese, onion, green peppers, garlic powder, and salt and pepper to taste. Stir in zucchini and bake in greased baking dish for 35 minutes. Let stand for 10 minutes before serving.

Easy Scalloped Potatoes

2 potatoes, thinly sliced with skins on   1 onion, chopped
4 bacon slices cooked and crumbled   1 cup cheddar cheese, grated
1 can cream of mushroom or celery soup

Boil potatoes in salted water until tender but firm. Drain. Cook bacon and chopped onions until tender; drain and crumble bacon. Simmer soup and ½ cup of cheese in a saucepan until cheese melts. Add sliced potatoes, bacon, and onions until heated through. Pour into baking dish, top with remaining cheese, and broil for 2 to 3 minutes or until golden brown.

Perfect Rice

Pour desired amount of rice into saucepan. Fill slowly with hot water until it is one knuckle deep above rice. Cook, uncovered, over medium heat until pocks form in rice. Remove from heat. Cover with tight lid, and let stand for 15 minutes. Rice will be tender and perfectly steamed.

Oriental Fried Rice

1 tbsp. olive oil   ½ cup onion, chopped
1 cup cold rice, cooked   1 egg, beaten
1 tbsp. soy sauce   ¼ tsp. salt
1 cup veggies

Cook onion in oil until tender, stirring constantly. Add rice and sauté. Beat egg, soy sauce, and salt. Add to rice mixture, stirring constantly. Add chopped veggies (broccoli, cauliflower, carrots, peas). Cook until tender.

Spicy Rice and Beans

1 cup rice, uncooked

1 ½ cups water

¼ cup onion, diced

2 tbsp. fresh cilantro, diced

¼ tsp. chili powder

½ cup cheddar cheese, grated

¼ cup guacamole

2 tbsp. olive oil

1 pint spicy stewed tomatoes

2 tbsp. green chilies, canned

¼ tsp. cumin

1 can pinto beans

¼ cup sour cream

Cook rice in oil, stirring constantly until grains are golden brown. In a saucepan, heat stewed tomatoes, onion, chilies, cilantro, cumin, and chili powder to a boil. Add rice; boil for 10 minutes. Cover and simmer for 15 to 20 minutes or until tender. Pour pinto beans in another saucepan, warm through, mash ½ of the beans, stir, and top with grated cheese. Serve rice and beans with a dollop of sour cream and guacamole.

Easy Chicken Cordon Bleu

4 boneless, skinless chicken breasts

1 egg

1 egg white

1/3 cup parmesan cheese, shredded

4 slices ham

1 tbsp. water

½ cup Seasoned Croutons, crushed

4 slices swiss cheese

Beat egg, egg white, and water in a shallow bowl. Combine parmesan cheese and crushed croutons together in a bag. Dip each chicken breast into egg mixture then toss in the bag and shake well to coat. Place chicken in a lightly greased baking dish and bake at 350°F for 30 minutes. Place 1 slice of ham and swiss cheese on each breast and return to the oven until cheese melts.

Swiss Vegetable Casserole

1 cup red potatoes, unpeeled and quartered
2 cups broccoli florets
1 cup cauliflower florets
½ cup carrots, shredded or curled
2 tsp. butter
1 cup fresh mushrooms, sliced
1 cup milk
½ cup swiss cheese, grated
½ tsp. salt
¼ tsp. black pepper
¼ tsp. hot pepper sauce
1/8 tsp. nutmeg
¼ cup parmesan cheese, grated

Bring potatoes to a boil, reduce heat, cover, and simmer for 10 minutes. Add broccoli, cauliflower, and carrots. Cover and cook 5 to 8 minutes or until veggies are tender. Drain and set aside. Melt butter in a saucepan, add mushrooms, and cook for 2 minutes, stirring constantly. Stir in flour and gradually stir in milk until thickened. Remove from heat. Add swiss cheese; stir until melted. Stir in salt, pepper, hot sauce, and nutmeg.

Preheat broiler. In greased baking dish, put veggies in and pour sauce over veggies. Top with parmesan cheese. Broil for a few minutes until cheese browns.

Beef Hash

1 cup beef broth or gravy
1 onion, diced
salt and pepper
garlic and onion powder

2 cups shredded raw potatoes
2 ½ cups cooked roast beef, diced
bacon drippings or butter

Combine broth, potatoes, onion, beef, and seasonings and mix well. In ovenproof skillet, add drippings until melted. Add meat mixture, cover, and simmer 25 to 30 minutes or until potato and onion are tender and hash is lightly browned underneath. Uncover and place in oven at 350°F for 15 to 20 minutes. To serve, fold hash in half like an omelet and slide onto heated platter. Serves 6. Bacon drippings are key to true hash.

Cheesy Spanish Rice

½ lb. lean ground beef	¼ cup chopped onion
¼ cup green peppers	¼ tsp. salt
1 cup cooked rice	½ cup shredded cheddar cheese
1 can tomato sauce	½ tsp. garlic powder

Brown beef with onion and green peppers; drain off fat. Add spices; stir in rice and cheese. Pour in tomato sauce and heat through. Serves 4 to 5.

Build a Pizza from Scratch

Dough

1 pkg. yeast	1 cup lukewarm water
1 tsp. sugar	½ tsp. salt
2 tbsp. olive oil	3 cups flour

Combine yeast, water, and sugar in large bowl and let set in warm place until bubbly. Add remaining ingredients and beat with spoon. Knead a few times. Grease bowl, put in dough, turn over once, and let rise in warm place until double in size.

Sauce

In a saucepan, combine ¾ tsp. oregano, ¾ tsp. rosemary, salt and pepper, ½ cup chopped black olives, 1 tsp. garlic powder, ½ onion chopped, ½ green pepper chopped, and a few mushrooms. Simmer.

Cheeses

Grate provolone, mozzarella, romano and Scamorza, about 2 cups each. Roll Dough out to fit in greased pizza pans. Spread sauce on dough, top with favorite meat if wanted, and add cheese. Bake at 400°F for 20 minutes or until cheese is melted and crust is golden brown. Makes 2 pizza pies.

Easy Lasagna

1 lb. Italian sausage	3 cans tomato sauce
1 box lasagna noodles	1 tub ricotta cheese
parsley, basil, oregano	fresh garlic, salt, pepper

Mix tomato sauce and spices. Remove skins from sausage and brown. Add to sauce. Cook noodles partially; slice ricotta cheese thinly. Layer meat, sauce, noodles, and cheese in a baking dish.

Bake at 375°F for 35 to 55 minutes. Serve with parmesan cheese, Italian bread, and a salad.

Baked Beans

1 lb. navy beans	½ lb. bacon (unsliced) or salt pork
1 tbsp. vinegar	½ tsp. dry mustard
½ cup dark molasses or Karo	salt to taste
1 cup chili sauce	1 onion, sliced
2 cups hot bean liquid	

Wash beans; cover with water 2 inches above beans. Soak overnight. Add bacon or salt pork. Cover. Simmer over low heat for about 1 hour; do not boil. Drain, reserve bean liquid. Remove meat. Cut into 1-inch cubes.

Pour beans into pot, mix in meat. Add remaining ingredients. Cover and bake slow at 300°F for 6 hours; may need to add more water.

Hamburger Helper

1 lb. lean ground beef

2 ¼ cup instant rice

¼ cup soy sauce

3 ½ cup hot water

2 tbsp. dry minced onion

Brown meat, drain fat. Add hot water, rice, onion, and soy sauce. Mix well, and bring to a boil. Cook slowly 10 to 15 minutes.

Corned Beef Hash

1 can corned beef

1 onion

salt and pepper

4 potatoes

butter

Slice onion and sauté in butter. Add peeled and cubed potatoes, 1 cup water, and salt and pepper to taste. Simmer covered for about 5 minutes. Crumble corned beef over the top. Mix well. Continue to cook until potatoes are tender.

Quick Refried Beans

3 cups cooked pinto beans

¼ cup oil

salt and pepper to taste

½ tsp. cumin powder

Mix beans and spices by hand until creamy. Fry in oil until heated through.

Stove Top Stuffing

10 bread ends

1 stalk celery, chopped

1 small onion, diced

¼ tsp. marjoram

¼ tsp. pepper

3 tbsp. butter

½ tsp. sage

2 cloves garlic, minced

2 tbsp. fresh chopped parsley

1 cup boiling water

Dice bread ends and measure bout 4 cups or so. Sauté celery, onion, and garlic in butter over medium heat for about 5 minutes. Add parsley, herbs, and pepper to sautéed veggie mix and stir. Add boiling water and bring to a boil. Remove from heat. Fork in bread, cover the pot, and let stand for 5 minutes. Serves 6.

Beef-a-Roni

1 lb. lean ground beef	2 cups elbow macaroni
salt and pepper	1 qt. stewed tomatoes
1 can tomato sauce	

Brown meat and drain well. Cook macaroni in salted water; drain. Add beef to macaroni; mix well. Add crushed stewed tomatoes, tomato sauce, and stir well. Add salt and pepper to taste. Simmer for 5 to 10 minutes on low heat.

Party Recipes

Mexican Bean Dip... page 79

Caramel Corn... page 81

Five-Cheeses Cheese Balls... page 80

Party Mix... page 82

Vegetable Garden Dip

1 cup sour cream
¼ cup fresh spinach, chopped

¼ cup parmesan cheese
1 pkg. dry onion soup mix

Mix together and serve.

Mexican Bean Dip

Layer 1	1 large can refried beans
Layer 2	1 lb. lean ground beef, browned in dry taco seasoning
Layer 3	1 large sour cream and 1 small jar of salsa
Layer 4	1 lb. cheddar cheese, grated

Bake at 350°F until bubbly. Cool before eating. Serve with nacho chips. For variations, add chopped onion and black olives.

Ranch Dip

2 cups sour cream   2 tbsp. ranch powder mix

Mix well and chill before serving.

Salmon or Shrimp Cheese Balls

2 cans shrimp or salmon   1 tbsp. horseradish
¼ tsp. salt   2 tbsp. grated onion
1 tbsp. lemon juice   18 oz. soft cream cheese
chopped walnuts

Mix first 5 ingredients well then add cheese. Chill overnight and the next day, form into balls and roll in chopped nuts.

Chicken Cheese Ball

1 cup cooked chicken, diced   3 tbsp. buttermilk
ranch powder   16 oz. cream cheese, soft
walnuts, chopped

Blend chicken, buttermilk, ranch powder, and cream cheese. Chill overnight. The next day, form into balls and roll in nuts.

Five-Cheeses Cheese Balls

16 oz. cream cheese
1 jar bacon cheese spread
1 jar Roka cheese spread
2 cups cheddar cheese, grated
8 oz. smoky cheddar cheese, grated
2 tsp. lemon juice
1 tbsp. worcestershire sauce
1 tbsp. minced onion
1 tbsp. minced green peppers
2 garlic buttons, minced
6 ea. black and green olives, sliced
walnuts, chopped
dash of salt

Mix cheeses well and add lemon juice and sauce. Add remaining ingredients and chill overnight. Next day, form into balls and roll in chopped nuts. Makes 3 large balls.

Cheese Log

1 lb. grated cheddar cheese
3 tbsp. minced green peppers
3 stuffed green olives, chopped
½ cup crushed saltine crackers
½ tsp. salt walnuts, chopped
2 tbsp. minced onion
2 tbsp. chopped dill pickles
1 boiled egg, chopped
¼ cup butter

Cream together and roll in nuts. Chill overnight and form into balls.

Pepperoni Pizza Spread

2 cups cheddar cheese, grated
2 cups mozzarella cheese, grated

1 cup mayonnaise

1 cup pepperoni, chopped

mushrooms, chopped

½ cup green peppers, chopped

1 cup black olives, chopped

1 cup stuffed green olives, chopped

Combine all ingredients and top with cheese. Bake at 350°F for 25 minutes until edges are bubbly and lightly brown. Serve with crackers.

Roasted Pumpkin Seeds

1 qt. water

2 cups pumpkin seeds

2 tbsp. salt

1 tbsp. olive oil, garlic flavored

Preheat oven to 250°F. Pick through seeds and remove any cut seeds. Remove as much of the stringy fibers as possible. Bring water and salt to a boil. Add seed and boil for 10 minutes. Drain and spread on paper towel to dry. Place seeds in a bowl with oil and toss to coat. Place on cookie sheet and roast for 40 minutes, stirring every 10 minutes. Cool the seeds and eat or pack in airtight containers and refrigerate until ready to eat.

Caramel Corn

2 cups sugar

½ cup Karo syrup

1 cup butter

1 tsp. salt

½ tsp. soda

1 tsp. vanilla

6 qts. popped corn

peanuts

Bring sugar, Karo, butter, and salt to a boil for 5 minutes. Stir in soda and vanilla. Pour over popped corn; stir to coat. In large roaster pan, bake at 250°F for 1 hour uncovered. Stir every 10 minutes. Add nuts and serve.

Party Mix

2 cups rice cereal

2 cups wheat cereal

2 cups corn cereal

2 cups oat cereal

1 cup pretzels

1 cup mixed nuts

1 cup cheesy crackers

1 lb. butter

3 tbsp. worcestershire sauce

¾ tsp. garlic powder

1 ½ tsp. seasoned salt

½ tsp. onion powder

2 cups raisins

2 cups dried cranberries and cherries, mixed

In a saucepan, melt butter and add sauce and spices. In roasting pan, combine cereal, nuts, and crackers. Drizzle butter sauce over and coat well. Roast for 15 minutes at 250°F. Remove from oven; mix in dried fruits. Spread over paper towel to cool. Makes 15 cups.

Granny's Favorite

Bread Recipes

Biscuits... page 86

Banana Bread... page 84

Strawberry Shortcake Biscuits... page 95

Corn Bread... page 90

Breadsticks

1 pkg. yeast	1 tsp. salt
1 tsp. cracked black pepper	2 cups flour
½ cup shortening	½ cup water
1 egg	

Place yeast, salt, pepper, and 1 cup flour in bowl. In a saucepan over low heat, place shortening and ½ cup water until warm and shortening is completely melted. Beat liquid into dry ingredients until well mixed for about 3 minutes. With wooden spoon, stir in other cup of flour and knead for 3 minutes. Set aside to rise to double in size for about 2 hours. Turn bread onto floured board and divide into fourths. Divide each fourth into 12 pieces. With hand, roll each piece until 12-inch rope is formed. Twist 2 ropes together loosely. Place on greased cookie sheet all 24 sticks. Beat egg and brush over breadsticks. Bake at 350°F for 25 minutes. Store in tightly covered container.

Basic Bread and Dinner Rolls

Preheat oven to 425°F. Mix together 1 pkg. yeast and ¼ cup warm water and set aside. Scald 1 ¾ cup milk and melt ½ cup butter. Let cool. Add 2 eggs, 1 ½ tsp. salt, and ½ cup sugar and mix well. Cool completely and stir in yeast mixture. Stir in 5 ½ to 6 cups flour and knead for 5 to 8 minutes. Cover and let rise in warm place for about 2 hours. (For loaves of bread, punch down, get all air out and form into 2 loaves, put in greased loaf pans, and bake.) For dinner rolls, punch down, get all air out, and roll in palm-sized balls for about 2 inches.

Put in greased pan and let rise for about 45 minutes. Bake for 10 minutes or until golden brown. Makes about 2 dozen rolls or 2 loaves of bread.

Banana Bread

½ cup shortening	1 cup sugar
2 eggs	1 cup mashed ripe bananas
1 tsp. lemon juice	2 cups sifted flour
3 tsp. baking powder	½ tsp. salt
1 cup chopped nuts (optional)	

Cream shortening and sugar, set aside. Beat eggs until light and add bananas and lemon juice. Blend in with shortening mixture. Sift flour, baking powder, and salt together and mix fast into banana mix. Add nuts. Bake in greased loaf pan at 375°F about 1 hour.

Honey Whole Wheat Bread

4 cups whole wheat flour	½ cup dry milk
1 tsp. salt	2 pkg. yeast
3 cup water	½ cup honey
2 tbsp. oil	4 cups flour

Combine 3 cups whole wheat flour, dry milk, yeast, and salt. Heat water, honey, and oil until warm and then add to flour mix with mixer. By hand, add rest of whole wheat flour and white flour. Knead for 5 minutes. Place in greased bowl and let rise until double in size. Divide into 2 loaves, cover, and let rise again. Bake for 30 to 35 minutes at 375°F. Makes 2 loaves.

Oatmeal Bread

Combine 1 ½ cup boiling water, 1 cup rolled oats, and 2 tbsp. shortening. Let cool. Add 2 tsp. salt, 1 pkg. yeast, ¾ cup warm water, 1 tsp. sugar. Add ¼ cup brown sugar, ¼ cup molasses, 3 ½ to 5 cups flour. Knead until smooth on floured surface. Place in greased bowl, cover, and let rise about 1 hour. Punch down and divide into 2 loaves. Let rise and then bake at 375°F for 30 to 35 minutes.

Zucchini Bread

4 eggs	3 cups sugar
2 cups grated zucchini	1 tsp. lemon juice
1 cup oil	3 1/4 cups flour
1 1/2 tsp. salt	1/3 cup water
1 cup raisins	1 tsp. cinnamon
1 tsp. nutmeg	2 tsp. baking soda
1 cup chopped nuts	

Mix all dry ingredients together then add remaining until well blended. Pour into 2 greased loaf pans and bake at 350°F for 1 hour.

Biscuits

2 cups sifted flour
1 tbsp. baking powder
1 tsp. salt
¾ cup milk (add ¼ cup for drop biscuits)
1/3 cup shortening

Sift together dry ingredients. Cut in shortening until crumbly. Add milk until dough forms. Roll out dough and cut biscuits (or drop by heaping spoonful) onto greased baking sheet. Bake at 375°F for 15 minutes or until golden brown.

Raisin Bread

2 pkgs. dry yeast
3 tbsp. sugar
1 1/3 cups milk
1 ½ tsp. salt
2 eggs, beaten
2 tbsp. butter

½ cup warm water
2/3 cup shortening
½ cup sugar
6 cups flour
1 cup raisins

Dissolve yeast in warm water. Stir in 3 tbsp. sugar then let stand 5 minutes. Combine shortening, milk, ½ cup sugar, and salt in a saucepan and heat until shortening melts. Remove from heat. Cool to lukewarm. Combine yeast mix to shortening mix, 2 cups flour, and eggs in large bowl. Beat well with mixer. Gradually stir in enough flour to make a soft dough. Turn dough onto flour board and work in raisins and knead until smooth. Place in greased bowl, cover, and let rise for 1 hour. Punch down dough and divide into 2 loaf pans. Let rise again. Bake in 350°F for 25 minutes.

Berry Nut Loaf

¾ cup butter   ¾ cup sugar
1 tsp. vanilla   4 eggs
2 cups flour   1 cup rolled oats
2 tsp. baking powder   1 tsp. salt
1 cup berry preserves   ½ cup sour cream
½ cup chopped nuts

Preheat oven to 350°F. Grease and flour loaf pan. In large pan, beat together butter, sugar, and vanilla until light and fluffy. Add eggs, one at a time, beating well after each addition.

In a medium bowl, combine flour, oats, baking powder, and salt.

In a small bowl, combine preserves and sour cream. Add dry ingredients alternately with preserves mixture to butter mixture, mixing until well blended. Stir in nuts; pour into prepared pan. Bake for about 45 minutes; tent bread with foil. Continue to bake for 25 to 30 minutes or until wooden toothpick inserted in center comes out clean. Cool for 10 minutes; remove from pan. Cool on wire rack. Makes 1 loaf.

Peach Bread

3 eggs, beaten   1 cup oil
2 ½ cup sugar   1 tsp. vanilla
1 tbsp. cinnamon   2 cups peaches, mashed
3 cups flour   1 tsp. each of salt, soda, and baking powder
½ cup nuts, chopped

Mix eggs, oil, sugar, vanilla, cinnamon, and peaches, blending each ingredient well before adding the next. Add flour, salt, soda, and baking powder and mix until well blended. Add chopped nuts and pour into well-greased and floured 2 loaf pans.

Sprinkle topping ½ cup brown sugar and ½ cup chopped nuts on top, and bake at 325°F for 45 to 60 minutes.

Cheese Rolls

3 cups flour	1 tbsp. dry minced onion
2 pkgs. yeast	1 tbsp. sugar
1 tsp. salt	½ tsp. celery seed, crushed
1 cup milk	½ cup water
2 tbsp. shortening	1 egg
1 cup shredded cheddar cheese	

Preheat oven to 400°F. In a large bowl, combine 2 cups flour, yeast, sugar, onion, salt, and celery seed and mix well. In a saucepan, heat milk and water until warm; add shortening, no need to melt. Add to flour mixture the egg; blend until moistened. Beat for 3 minutes and add cheese. By hand, gradually stir in enough flour to make a stiff batter. Cover and let rise in warm place until light and doubled in size for about 30 minutes. Stir down batter and spoon into greased muffin cups. Cover and let rise in warm place until doubled again for about 30 minutes. Bake for 20 minutes or until golden brown. Serve warm.

Cheese Puffs

¼ cup butter	½ cup flour
¼ lb. cheese, grated	

Preheat oven to 350°F. Mix all well and roll into small balls about the size of marbles. Bake on an ungreased cookie sheet for 15 to 20 minutes.

Cinnamon Puffs

1 pkg. yeast	¼ cup warm water
½ cup milk, scalded and cooled	1/8 cup sugar
¼ tsp. salt	¼ cup oil
1 egg, beaten	2 cups flour
1 ½ tsp. vanilla	¼ cup butter, melted
½ cup sugar	1 tbsp. cinnamon

In a large bowl, dissolve yeast in warm water. Set aside for 10 minutes. Stir in milk, sugar, salt, oil, egg, and 1 cup flour; mix well. Beat in additional flour and vanilla until dough is sticky. Spoon dough into greased muffin tins. Let rise until doubled in size for about 1 hour. Preheat oven to 375°F. Bake for 15 to 20 minutes or until golden brown. Place melted butter in small bowl. Mix sugar and cinnamon in another small bowl. Remove rolls from tin and dip first in melted butter then in sugar and cinnamon mix.

Hamburger Buns

2 pkgs. yeast	¼ cup sugar
½ cup warm water	6 cups sifted flour
½ cup nonfat dry milk	1 tbsp. salt
2 cups water	2 eggs, beaten
½ cup oil	2 eggs, beaten
¼ cup milk	sesame or poppy seeds

Preheat oven to 425°F. Combine yeast, sugar, and warm water. Let stand until yeast is softened. Stir until dissolved. In a large bowl, sift together flour, dry milk, and salt. Make a well in the center of dry ingredients. Pour in water, yeast mixture, eggs, and oil. Mix well. Cover, let rise in warm place for 1 hour. Turn dough on floured board, turning to coat well. Pinch off pieces about the size of an egg. Place smooth side upon a greased baking sheet 3 inches apart. Brush with beaten egg and milk mixture. Sprinkle with seeds, optional. Let rise for 20 minutes. Bake for 8 to 12 minutes. Makes 30 buns.

Corn Bread

1 cup yellow cornmeal	1 cup flour
¼ cup sugar	½ tsp. salt
4 tsp. baking powder	1 egg, beaten
1 cup milk	¼ cup oil

Preheat oven to 425°F. Mix all until well blended. Pour into greased 8"× 8" baking pan and bake for 20 minutes or until lightly golden or until knife comes out clean.

Pizza Dough

½ cup warm water	1 tbsp. yeast
1/3 cup oil	1 cup flour
1 tsp. garlic salt	½ cup cornmeal

Preheat oven to 425°F. Dissolve yeast in water and let stand for 10 minutes. Add oil. Mix in flour, garlic salt, and cornmeal. Mix until combined, soft, but not stiff. Form into ball and roll out. Place on greased pizza pan or pie plan. Gently pull dough out to edges. Poke with fork randomly. Bake crust for 10 minutes. Spread on sauce and favorite toppings. (Meat should already be cooked.) Top with cheese. Place in oven for 10 minutes longer or until done.

Wheat Pizza Crust

1 egg, beaten	¼ cup oil
2/3 cup warm water	½ cup cornmeal
1 ½ cups whole wheat flour	1 tsp. salt
1 tsp. baking powder	2 tsp. garlic powder

Preheat oven to 425°F. Mix egg, oil, and water and set aside. In large bowl, combine flour, cornmeal, salt, baking powder, and garlic powder. Pour liquid mixture into flour mixture. By hand, blend well. Form into ball and press onto greased pizza pan. Bake for 10 minutes and top with sauce, toppings, and cheese then bake for 10 to 20 minutes or until done.

Early American Brown Bread

2 cups whole wheat flour

2 tsp. baking soda

½ tsp. salt

4 tsp. vinegar

¾ cup white flour

1 cup packed brown sugar

2 cups milk

Preheat oven to 350°F. In large bowl, mix wheat flour, white flour, soda, brown sugar, and salt. In a small bowl, combine milk and vinegar. Let stand for ten minutes. Stir in milk mix gradually into flour mix until well blended. Spoon batter into greased loaf pan. Bake for 1 hour.

Spiced Pumpkin Bread

1 ¾ cups flour

1 tsp. baking soda

½ tsp. nutmeg

1 ½ cups sugar

½ cup oil

½ cup nuts, chopped

¼ tsp. salt

½ tsp. cinnamon

1 cup cooked pumpkin

2 eggs, beaten

½ cup water

1 cup raisins

For variation, chocolate chips may be substituted for raisins.

Preheat oven to 350°F. In a bowl, sift flour, salt, soda, cinnamon, and nutmeg. In another bowl, combine pumpkin, sugar, eggs, oil, and water. Beat into flour mix. Fold in nuts and raisins or chocolate chips. Pour into greased loaf pan and bake for 1 hour.

Buttermilk Oatmeal Muffins

1 cup milk	2 tsp. vinegar
1 cup instant oats	1/3 cup butter
½ cup brown sugar, packed	1 egg, beaten
1 cup flour	1 tsp. salt
½ tsp. baking soda	1 tsp. baking powder
¾ cup raisins	½ cup nuts

Preheat oven to 400°F. Combine milk and vinegar. Soak oatmeal in milk for 30 minutes. Cream together butter, sugar, and egg. Sift flour, salt, baking powder, and soda. Stir into creamed mix. Stir in raisins and chopped nuts just until moistened. Stir in oatmeal mixture. Spoon into greased muffin tins. Bake for 20 minutes.

Basic Muffin Mix

2 cups flour, sifted	1 tbsp. baking powder
½ tsp. salt	3 tbsp. sugar
1 egg, beaten	1 cup milk
3 tbsp. oil	

Preheat oven to 450°F. Sift together flour, baking powder, salt, and sugar. Combine egg, milk, and oil. Pour into dry ingredients. Stir only until moist. Do not over mix. Spoon batter into greased muffin tins, filling cups about 2/3 full. Bake for 20 to 25 minutes.

Muffin Variations

Apple Nutmeg. Peel and dice one apple. Sprinkle with 1 tsp. nutmeg and 2 tsp. sugar. Stir into batter.

Apricot Nut. Drain ½ cup cooked, pitted, and chopped apricots. Combine with ½ cup chopped walnuts. Stir into batter.

Cheese Garlic. Combine 1 cup grated cheese with 1/8 tsp. garlic salt. Stir well into dry ingredients then add egg, milk, and oil.

Lemon Sugar. Combine ½ cup sugar with 2 tbsp. grated lemon peel. Fill tins to ¼ full with batter. Sprinkle with sugar mixture then top with batter to fill 2/3 full.

Berries. Drain ¾ cup washed berries. Add ¼ cup sugar and 1/8 tsp. cinnamon. Gently fold into muffin batter.

Carrots. Add ½ cup shredded carrots to dry ingredients.

Jam or Preserves. Fill muffin tins ¼ full with batter. Put 1 tsp. jam in middle and top with batter to 2/3 full.

Orange. Use only ¾ cup milk and add ¼ cup orange juice. Grate 1 tbsp. of orange peel and stir into liquid ingredients. Mix in dry ingredients.

Biscuit and Baking Mix

8 ¾ cups flour	1/3 cup baking powder
¼ cup sugar	1 tbsp. salt
2 cups butter or shortening	

In a very large bowl, mix together all dry ingredients with wire whisk. Cut in butter until crumbly. Store in large airtight container until ready to use. Use with some of these variations below.

Biscuits. With 2 cups mix, make hole in center. Add ½ cup liquid (milk, water, or half milk and half water). Work in quickly with fork just until dough follows fork around 20 to 40 seconds. Turn out onto floured board; knead gently about 10 folds. Roll out ½-inch thick and cut into rounds. Bake on ungreased baking sheet at 450°F for 12 to 15 minutes.

Drop Biscuits. Increase liquid to 2/3 cup.

Cheese Biscuits. Add 1/3 cup grated cheese.

Onion Biscuits. Add ¼ cup chopped sautéed onion.

Ham or Bacon Biscuits. Add 1/3 cup crisp bacon or ¼ cup finely chopped ham.

Pancakes. Add 1 1/3 cups milk and 1 egg to 2 cups of mix. Beat smooth. Fold in ½ cup blueberries or ¾ cup sliced apples. Drop ¼ mix in hot, lightly greased griddle. Makes 10 (4-inch) pancakes.

Shortcakes. With fork, lightly beat 1 egg in bowl. Add ½ cup milk, 3 tbsp. sugar, and 3 cups of lightly spooned mix. Mix quickly with for, turn out on floured board, and knead well 8 times. Roll out to ½-inch thick cut in rounds as desired. Brush a round with melted butter and stack with another. Makes 5 or 6 double shortcakes. Bake at 425°F for 12 to 15 minutes.

Quick Muffins. To 3 cups of mix, add 3 tbsp. sugar. Beat 1 egg with 1 cup milk. Pour into greased muffin tins 2/3 full and bake at 400°F for 20 minutes.

Blueberry. Fold in 1 cup fresh, frozen, or canned and drained blueberries.

Cranberry. Add 1 tbsp. sugar and ¾ cup cranberries.

Applesauce. Use only 2/3 cup milk plus ½ cup applesauce and a few dashes of cinnamon.

Pocket Bread

2 ¼ cups warm water
1 pkg. yeast
2 tsp. salt
4 ½ cups flour

1 tsp. sugar
1 tbsp. oil
1 cup gluten flour

Combine ¼ cup water, sugar, yeast in large bowl until frothy for about 10 minutes. Beat in remaining water, oil, and salt. Beat in gluten flour vigorously for 3 minutes. Gradually add other flour until too stiff to beat. Turn out and knead well. Form into a 14-inch-long log. Cut into 14 slices, and lay slices 3 inches apart on floured board. Cover with dry towel then wet towel and let rise for about 1 hour. On a floured surface, roll each piece into a 6-inch round. Sprinkle baking sheet with cornmeal and lay rounds on them and let rise for 30 minutes. Preheat oven to 475°F. Put one pan on as low as you can for 4 ½ minutes. Then transfer it to upper shelf and put another pan on bottom for 4 ½ minutes. Keep this up until all have been on bottom for 4 ½ minutes and upper shelf for 4 ½ minutes. Stack in towels and cool.

Strawberry Shortcake Biscuits

2 cups flour
4 tsp. baking powder
½ cup butter
2/3 cup milk

3 tbsp. sugar
½ tsp. salt
1 egg, beaten

Mix all and pat out on floured board. Cut ¾ inch thick. Bake on ungreased sheet at 450°F for 10 to 14 minutes. Serve with sweetened berries and whipped cream.

Pita Bread

1 pkg. yeast	1 ¼ cups warm water
3 cups flour	2 tsp. salt

Dissolve yeast in warm water. Stir in flour and salt. Stir into a rough sticky ball. Knead on floured board until smooth, adding more flour if necessary. Divide into 6 balls. Knead each until smooth and round. Flatten each until ¼-inch thick and 4 to 5 inches around. Cover with towel and let rise for 45 minutes. Arrange the rounds upside down on baking sheet. Bake at 400°F for 10 to 15 minutes or until browned and puffed in center. They will be hard to remove from oven, but they will soften and flatten as they cool. For sandwiches, split carefully and fill with sandwich makings.

Flour Tortillas

2 cups flour	1 tsp. baking powder
½ tsp. salt	4 tsp. shortening
½ cup water	

Mix well and rest for 10 minutes. Knead for 5 minutes. Rest for 10 minutes. Make into 8 balls, let rest for 10 minutes. Pat flat, roll into circles. Place in a medium-hot skillet briefly then turn with spatula. Remove from heat. Store in plastic bag in refrigerator until ready to use.

Soft Taco Shells

flour cornmeal	1 egg
salt	pepper

Mix ingredients well, should be very thin. Spoon mixture onto hot flat skillet, spreading into a round shape. Fry until lightly browned on both sides. Keep warm in oven until ready to serve. Serve buttered as taco shells or in enchiladas.

Specialty Bread

½ cup milk	1 ½ cup water
4 tbsp. butter	1 pkg. yeast
7 cups flour	1 tbsp. seasoned salt
1 tbsp. garlic salt	1 medium onion, chopped
2 tbsp. olive oil	

In a saucepan, heat milk and water until very warm. Set aside and add yeast and butter until yeast dissolves. In mixing bowl, mix half of the flour, the salts, and the onion. Pour in the yeast mixture, slowly stirring constantly. Knead thoroughly while adding additional flour until smooth. Brush with olive oil. Cover and let rise in warm place for 30 minutes. Bake for 20 to 25 minutes at 375°F.

For Italian Bread. Substitute 2 tbsp. Italian seasoning and ½ cup romano or parmesan cheese for onion.

For Cheese Bread. Substitute ½ cup grated cheddar and ½ cup Monterey-Jack cheese for onion. Sprinkle with cornmeal then bake.

Croissant

¾ cup warm water	2 pkgs. active dry yeast
½ cup sour cream	3 ½ cups flour, divided
2 tbsp. sugar	1 ½ cups butter
1 tsp. salt	1 egg
1 tbsp. water	

To Make Dough. Pour water in bowl, sprinkle in yeast. Stir to dissolve. Add sour cream, ½ cup flour, and sugar. Blend with whisk until smooth. Cover and let rest in warm place for about 2 hours. Slice butter into ½-inch pats. In a bowl, gently toss with remaining flour and salt. When all pats are well coated, slightly flatten each one between fingers. Refrigerate. Pour yeast mixture into flour/butter mix. Stir until moist. (Dough will be course.) On lightly floured board, pat into 10-inch squares (avoid overworking). Roll dough with floured rolling pin into 18"× 12" rectangle. Dough will still be coarse.

To Fold Dough. Slip a flat cookie sheet under third of dough. Fold this section of dough over center third section. Repeat with other section so dough is folded into equal thirds. Repeat folding and folding procedure. Place dough on flour plate, cover with plastic wrap, and chill for 30 minutes. Repeat folding and rolling procedure 3 more times. (If butter softens, chill for 30 minutes.) Wrap dough in plastic wrap and chill for at least 2 hours up to 24 hours.

Shaping Croissants. Cut dough into 4 equal sections; work with each section one at a time. On lightly floured board, roll into an 8"× 12" rectangle. Cut into 3 triangles. To form fourth triangle, press leftover side pieces together, overlapping slightly. Make a 1-inch slit at base of 1 triangle. Loosely roll dough on both sides of slit up to top of slit, angling rolls slightly outward as well. (This prevents croissant from becoming too thick.) Continue rolling to pointed tip. Curve ends to form crescent shape. Place on ungreased cookie sheet. Repeat with other 3 triangles, and place 3 inches apart. Repeat shaping with remaining dough. Cover cookie sheet loosely with plastic wrap. Let rise in warm place for 2 hours or until doubled.

Preheat oven at 450°F. Mix egg with water, and brush croissants. Bake for 13 to 15 minutes.

Cinnamon Walnut Scones

Combine 1 ¾ cup flour, ¼ cup chopped walnuts, 4 ½ tsp. sugar, 2 ¼ tsp. baking powder, ½ tsp. salt, and ½ tsp. cinnamon. Cut in ¼ cup cold butter. Add 2 eggs and 1/3 cup heavy cream. Stir until moistened. Pat into 7-inch circle, ¾-inch thick. Cut into 8 wedges. Place separate wedges on lightly greased baking sheet. Brush tops with ¼ cup buttermilk. Let rise for 15 minutes. Bake at 450°F for 14 to 16 minutes. Makes 8.

Raised Doughnuts

2 cups warm water	1 pkg. yeast
1 tsp. honey	2 eggs, beaten
¾ cup sugar	1 tsp. cinnamon
1 tsp. lemon extract	flour
1 stick melted butter	

Mix warm water, yeast, and honey in a large bowl. Cover with towel; let rise until bubbly. Add remaining ingredients. Add flour until it begins to lose stickiness. Cover with towel and let rise. Punch down. Roll out and cut out doughnuts. Place on floured cookie sheet and let rise. Fry top down first. Flip doughnuts immediately when they rise to the surface. Put them into sugar when done and eat. Freeze any not eaten the first day.

Potato Bread and Doughnuts

2 medium potatoes, cooked	½ cup sugar
2 tbsp. salt	4 tbsp. shortening
2 pkg. dry yeast	1 ½ pt. fluid-mashed potatoes and water

Mix with flour until stiff enough to knead. Knead until nice and elastic, for about 10 to 15 minutes. Let rise until double in size. Work out as rolls or loaves of bread. Let rise again then bake at 375°F for 25 to 30 minutes.

Doughnuts. After letting the dough rise, roll out until about ½-inch thick. Cut with doughnut cutter. Let rise until double in size. Fry in deep fat until brown on both sides. Drain on paper towels. Dip in honey, powdered sugar, cinnamon, or nutmeg.

Doughnuts

1 cup sugar
1 tsp. baking soda
2 eggs
1 cup sour milk
shortening

1 tbsp. nutmeg
½ tsp. salt
1 tbsp. shortening
6 cups flour

Mix sugar, nutmeg, soda, salt, eggs, milk, and shortening. Add enough flour to roll out dough and cut with doughnut cutter. Heat shortening to 375°F; drop doughnuts in, turning several times. Drain on soft crumpled paper. Cool and dust with powdered sugar if desired.

Note: milk can be soured by adding 1 tbsp. vinegar to 1 cup fresh milk.

Doughnuts

1 cup boiling water
½ cup sugar
1 can evaporated milk
1 pkg. yeast
1 tsp. salt

¼ cup shortening
2 eggs
1 tsp. vanilla
6 cups flour

Melt shortening in boiling water. Remove from heat, cool a bit, then add sugar, eggs, evaporated milk, and vanilla. Dissolve yeast in ¼ cup warm water. Add to liquid mixture; mix well. Add flour and salt. Let rise in warm place for 1 hour. Roll out on pastry cloth or floured surface. Cut doughnuts and let rise again. Fry in hot oil. Roll in powdered sugar, granulated sugar, or combination of both. Or drizzle with glaze: 1 cup powdered sugar, 2 tbsp. milk, splash of vanilla.

Quick Jelly Donuts

1 can of 10 refrigerated buttermilk biscuits   ½ cup melted butter

3 tbsp. sugar   1 tsp. cinnamon

1 cup jelly or jam

Preheat oven to 375°F. Place melted butter in a small bowl. In another small bowl, combine sugar and cinnamon. In another bowl, stir jelly until smooth. Prepare and bake biscuits according to package directions. Immediately from the oven, dip each hot biscuit into melted butter, coating all sides. Roll in sugar mixture, coating all sides. Make a slit through the side of each biscuit with a butter knife and fill with jelly.

Quick Cinnamon Rolls

2 ¼ cups biscuit mix (p. 93)   2/3 cup milk

¼ cup sugar   ½ cup raisins

1 ½ tsp. cinnamon   ¼ cup butter, melted

½ cup nuts, chopped

Preheat oven to 425°F. Beat biscuit mix and milk until dough is stiff. Knead on floured board until dough is smooth. Roll out into rectangle. Spread top with half of the melted butter; sprinkle with sugar, cinnamon, nuts, and raisins. Roll dough up tightly and press to seal. Cut into 10 slices. Place rolls close together on greased baking sheet. Brush with remaining melted butter and bake for 10 to 12 minutes or until golden brown. May drizzle top with glaze: 1 cup powdered sugar, 2 tbsp. milk, and a splash of vanilla.

Rich Buttermilk Biscuits

1 cup flour	½ tsp. salt
2 tsp. baking powder	1/8 tsp. baking soda
1/8 cup shortening	½ cup milk
1 tsp. lemon juice or vinegar	

Preheat oven to 450°F. Sift flour, salt, baking powder, and soda. Cut in shortening. Combine milk and lemon juice or vinegar. Stir into flour mixture to make soft dough. Turn dough onto floured board and knead until soft and elastic. Roll out to ½-inch thick and cut into biscuits. Bake on ungreased baking sheet for 8 to 10 minutes.

Pretzels

1 loaf bread dough (pp. 84, 91)
1 egg white, slightly beaten
1 tbsp. water
coarse salt

Roll out dough into square. Cut dough into 30 strips and roll each strip between palms into long rope. Shape into pretzels by tying in a loose knot and looping ends through; pinch to seal. Let stand for 30 minutes. Mix egg white and water and brush on pretzels and sprinkle with coarse salt. Bake on greased cookie sheet at 350°F. 15 to 18 minutes or until golden.

Granny's Favorite

Pasta Recipes

Soup Noodles... page 107

Ravioli... page 103

Potato Pasta... page 106

Ravioli

Pasta Dough

1 tsp. salt	2 eggs
2 tbsp. olive oil	1 cup water
flour	

On a board, form a circle with the flour. Add rest of ingredients in a well in center and mix together to form stiff dough. Knead for about 20 minutes then lightly flour a spot on the board. Put the ball of dough on it and cover with bowl. Let stand for 30 minutes. Knead for a few minutes and divide into 3 or 4 pieces. Place pieces in a bowl and cover while you roll out one piece. Roll very thin and crease the center with lightly floured board under it. Flip back top half and fill with stuffing to the crease, leaving slightly margin on end. Flip top piece back and press edges firmly. Mark and cut and lay out. Repeat until all dough is used.

Filling

4 boxes frozen leaf spinach	2 onions chopped
6 oz. cream cheese	½ cup grated parmesan cheese
1 lb. veal grinded finely	1 lb. pork ground finely (lean meat)
8 eggs	2 tbsp. chopped mushrooms
½ tsp. pepper	1 ½ tsp. salt
¼ tsp. garlic salt	1 cup cracker crumbs

Cook meat in 1 cup water for about 30 minutes and cool. Cook spinach, drain, and chop finely. Chop onions and mushrooms. In a bowl, mix all ingredients well. Add more salt and pepper if needed. Place in a bowl and cover with wax paper and a towel. If stiff when using, add a little water. Any unused filling can be frozen. Ravioli can be frozen raw or cooked.

Sicilian Pasta

2 eggs
pinch salt
2 cups sifted flour

Sift flour onto a wooden board. Make a well and drop 2 eggs into the well. Add salt. With hands, work the flour and egg mixture into dough, similar to bread dough. Clean and dust board lightly with flour and knead the dough for 5 to 10 minutes until the dough is smooth and elastic. Cut dough into 4 sections. Roll each section one at a time on a floured board with rolling pin until very thin. Cut into shapes you desire. Place pasta on a clean surface. If making a big batch, put a clean sheet on your bed and let dry there and it will dry fast. Homemade pasta cooks faster than commercial pasta.

German Pasta

4 large eggs
3 cups sifted flour

Mix eggs and flour together to make stiff dough. Knead by hand until dough starts to blister and form bubbles. Divide dough into 5 parts; roll out each part until paper thin on lightly floured board. Place on towel to dry until layers will not stick together, turning several times. Roll each layer into tight roll and slice very thinly. Loosen noodles and spread out on cloth to dry before using or storing.

Fettuccini Pasta

3 cups flour   ½ tsp. salt
3 eggs (may use egg beaters)   3 tbsp. olive oil
¼ cup water

Sift flour and salt into a large bowl. Make well at center of flour; add eggs, oil and water. Work liquids into flour by hand to make stiff dough. Knead dough for 10 minutes or until dough is soft and smooth. Cover with damp towel and let dough rest 20 minutes. Cut dough into 4 sections. Roll each quarter very thinly in rectangle shape. Fold each rolled-out dough into quarters lengthwise and slice dough across into ¼-inch-wide strips. Unwind strips and allow to dry on clean dry cloth for 1 hour or longer.

Spaghetti Pasta

Use 1 cup flour and 1 egg per person   This is for 8 people.

For 8 cups flour, add a small handful of salt. Make a well in the flour, adding eggs, and mix by hand. Add 2 cups of water gradually until dough is mixed well. It should be on the hard side, not soft. Knead on floured board and cover. Cut dough into manageable balls. Using one ball, cover remaining with cloth. Roll out dough into a large circle about ¼ to ½-inch thick. Cut into strips about 3 inches wide. Roll these through the flat roller of your spaghetti machine. You may have to cut them in half for a shorter length.

Potato Pasta

2 to 3 cups flour
¼ tsp. nutmeg
½ cup chopped parsley
1 ½ cups sliced mushrooms
2 tsp. salt
2 cups mashed potatoes
2 egg yolks
½ cup butter, melted

Combine potatoes and egg yolks. Add flour, salt, and nutmeg. Work mixture into a firm dough, adding more flour if necessary. Knead on a floured board until dough is smooth. Roll out dough to 1/16-inch thick. Cut pasta in narrow strips (may let dry for a while). Boil pasta in salted water for 7 minutes. Drain. Sauté mushrooms in butter for 3 minutes and add parsley. Toss mushrooms with pasta and season to taste. Serves 8.

Soup Noodles

1 cup flour
2 eggs
½ tsp. salt

Add milk to above just enough to keep dough thick. Roll flat with fork. Use enough flour so that dough does not stick to cutting board. Roll dough into a roll using a generous amount of flour. Cut rolled dough into noodle-size pieces. Place on cookie sheet and toss with additional flour (noodles must not stick to each other). Dry noodles. Place the amount of noodles needed into large pot of boiling water. Add salt. Boil until tender, drain. Use in soup or as a base dish with meat and various sauces. Noodles not used can be tossed with more flour and frozen.

Note: noodles should dry for 1 to 2 hours prior to using, tossing them with the flour for quicker drying.

Polish Pasta

3 cups flour   3 eggs
2 to 3 tbsp. water   1 tsp. salt

Sift flour onto a board. Make a well in center and place eggs, water, and salt in well. Work ingredients into a dough and knead until smooth for about 1 minute. Divide into 2 parts. Roll on floured board until very thin. Let dry for about an hour.

Granny's Favorite
Dessert Recipes

Old-Time Rice Pudding... page 110   Old-Fashioned Butter Cake... page 130   Perfect Pumpkin Pie... page 169

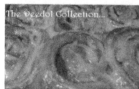

Grand Cinnamon Rolls... page 137   Chocolate Chip Cookies... page 152   Funnel Cakes... page 133

Building a Cobbler....page 125

Mincemeat Cake

9 oz. box mincemeat

2 ½ cups sugar

2 eggs

1 tsp. cinnamon

1 tsp. salt

½ cup walnuts

2 cups milk

1 cup shortening

1 tbsp. baking powder

½ tsp. allspice

3 ¼ cups flour

Crumble mincemeat into milk and soak well and set aside. Cream together sugar and shortening. Add eggs and beat well. Sift in baking powder, cinnamon, allspice, salt, and flour. Beat well. Add walnuts and mincemeat mix. Divide into two 9-inch greased and floured loaf pans. Bake at 350°F for 1 hour. Cool for 10 minutes and turn out.

Granny's Best Pie Crust

5 ½ cups flour	1 lb. butter
1 tsp. salt	1 egg
1 tbsp. vinegar	water to fill cup

Cut butter into flour and salt. In a cup, put egg and vinegar and fill to the top with water. Work into flour mixture. Roll into 6 balls of equal size. May wrap tightly with plastic wrap and freeze in airtight freezer bag what cannot be used right away. Makes 3 double crusts.

Layered Pudding Delight

14 graham crackers	1 pkg. Instant Vanilla pudding
2 cups cold milk	1 cup Cool Whip
1 can cherry pie filling	

Mix pudding with milk and Cool Whip. In 9"× 9" pan, layer crackers, next ½ of the vanilla pudding mixture, next crackers, next last ½ of pudding mixture, and top with cherry pie filling.

Bread Pudding

8 eggs (egg substitute can be used)
4 cups milk
2/3 cups sugar
1 tsp. cinnamon
1 tsp. vanilla
¼ tsp. salt

4 to 5 cups dry wheat bread crumbs (8 slices)
2/3 cup raisins

Beat together eggs, milk, sugar, cinnamon, vanilla, and salt. Place bread cubes in 10"× 10" baking dish. Sprinkle raisins over bread. Pour egg mixture over all. Chill overnight. Bake at 325°F for 40 to 45 minutes or until knife inserted comes out clean. Cool slightly. Serve warm with vanilla sauce (see below). Serves 8.

Vanilla Sauce

1 cup heavy cream
1 tsp. vanilla extract
1 tbsp. water

3 tbsp. sugar
2 tsp. cornstarch

Bring cream, sugar, and vanilla to a slow boil over medium heat. Do not burn. Mix cornstarch with water and add to saucepan. Cook for 3 minutes on simmer until thickened. May be made ahead, refrigerated and later warmed. Topping for bread pudding.

Old-Time Rice Pudding

½ cup rice
½ cup sugar
1 tsp. grated lemon peel
½ cup raisins

1 qt. milk
dash of salt
¼ tsp. nutmeg

Combine rice, milk, sugar, and salt. Pour into buttered 1 ½ quart baking dish. Bake at 300°F slowly for 1 hour; stir occasionally. Add lemon peel, nutmeg, and raisins. Continue baking for 1 ½ hours. Two-thirds cup brown sugar may be used in place of granulated sugar. Serves 6.

Creamy Rice Pudding

2 ½ cups water

dash salt

dash nutmeg

14 oz. sweetened condensed milk

½ cup uncooked long-grained rice

¼ tsp. cinnamon

2 pieces lemon rind ½"

additional cinnamon

Combine water, rice, salt, cinnamon, nutmeg, and lemon rind in a saucepan. Let stand for 30 minutes. Bring to a boil, stirring occasionally. Add sweetened condensed milk, return to a boil, and stir. Reduce heat and cook uncovered, stirring frequently for 20 to 25 minutes or until liquid is absorbed to top of rice. Cool; pudding will thicken while it cools. Remove lemon rind, and sprinkle with additional cinnamon. Serve warm or chilled. Refrigerate all leftovers.

Death by Chocolate Cake

1 devil's food chocolate cake mix

1 jar hot fudge ice cream sauce

1 pkg. chocolate pudding

1 bag mini chocolate chips

1 jar caramel ice cream sauce

whipped cream with chocolate powder

Mix cake according to directions on box. Pour into 9"× 13" cake pan (greased and floured); then add ½ cup chocolate chips. Bake for 15 minutes. Sprinkle chocolate chips, reserving ¾ cup, and continue to bake according to box instructions. Remove from oven when baked and poke holes with a wooden spoon in warm cake. Heat jars of fudge and caramel over low heat in water bath for them to be easy to pour.

Pour hot fudge sauce over cake. Pour caramel sauce over cake. Allow cake to cool; put in fridge. Mix chocolate pudding and whipped cream and frost cooled cake. Top with remaining chocolate chips.

Cream Cheese Frosting

8 oz. cream cheese, softened

2 tsp. vanilla

¼ to ½ cup cocoa powder (optional)

½ cup butter, softened

confectioners' sugar

Beat together all ingredients to desired consistency; spread on cooled cake.

Cocoa Cola Cake

1 white cake mix

2 eggs

½ cup butter

1 tsp. vanilla

1 cup regular Coke

½ cup buttermilk

¼ cup baking cocoa

1 ½ cup miniature marshmallows

Combine all ingredients except the marshmallows and beat for 2 minutes, then fold in marshmallows. Pour into a greased and floured 9"× 13" baking pan. Bake at 350°F for 35 to 40 minutes. Let stand 15 minutes to cool. Frost (see below) and serve.

Fudge Frosting

¼ cup baking cocoa

1/3 cup regular Coke

1 cup chopped walnuts or pecans

½ cup butter, cubed

4 cups powdered sugar

Combine cocoa and butter in a saucepan and cook over low heat until butter is melted. Stir in Coke until blended. Bring to a boil, stirring constantly. Remove from heat. Stir in powdered sugar until smooth. Fold in nuts and spread over cake. Let stand for 20 minutes before cutting.

Bonbons

2 cups powdered sugar

½ cup flour

½ cup butter

1 bag chocolate almond bark

1 cup graham cracker crumbs

½ cup flaked coconut

½ cup peanut butter

In a bowl, mix powdered sugar, graham crackers, flour, and coconut and set aside. In a saucepan, melt butter and peanut butter and pour over coconut mixture. Mix well until all is moist. Shape into 1-inch balls and dip in melted chocolate almond bark. Place on wax paper; store in fridge.

Peanut Butter Bonbons

1 ½ cups creamy peanut butter

1 tbsp. vanilla extract

14 oz. sweetened condensed milk

14 oz. chocolate or vanilla candy coating, melted

¾ cup butter, soft

1 tsp. salt

2 lbs. powdered sugar

In large bowl, beat peanut butter, butter, vanilla, and salt until fluffy. Gradually beat in sweetened condensed milk, next powdered sugar until smooth. Shape into 1-inch balls. Place on baking sheets. Chill until firm. Dip into melted candy coating, not coating completely. Place on wax paper; chill until firm. Store in fridge or freezer.

Peanut and Pretzel Bark

28 oz. chocolate- or vanilla-flavored candy coating or almond bark

1 ½ cups broken thin pretzels   1 cup coarsely chopped peanuts

In a saucepan, over low heat, melt candy coating or almond bark, stirring frequently. Remove from heat, and stir in pretzels and peanuts. Spread into thin layer on 2 wax paper–lined baking sheets. Chill for 30 minutes or until firm. Break into chunks. Store in fridge.

Quick Chocolate Mousse

14 oz. sweetened condensed milk   4 oz. instant chocolate pudding
1 cup cold water   1 cup whipping cream, whipped

In a bowl, combine sweetened condensed milk, pudding mix, and water. Beat until well blended. Chill for 5 minutes. Fold in whipped cream. Spoon into serving dishes and chill.

Creamy Banana Pudding

14 oz. sweetened condensed milk
1 ½ cups cold water
1 small pkg. vanilla instant pudding
2 cups whipped cream
36 vanilla wafers
3 medium bananas, sliced and dipped in lemon juice

In bowl, combine sweetened condensed and water. Add pudding mix, beat until well blended. Chill for 5 minutes. Fold in whipped cream. Spoon 1 cup pudding mixture into baking dish. Top with wafers, then bananas, and pudding. Repeat 2 more times, ending with pudding mixture. Chill and serve.

Maple Mousse

4 eggs   1 cup maple syrup
2 cups heavy cream   1 tsp. vanilla

Turn temperature control of fridge to coldest setting. Separate yolks and whites of eggs. Beat egg yolks lightly. Heat maple syrup using double boiler over hot, not boiling water. Stir in yolks. Cook and stir constantly until thickened for about 2 to 3 minutes. Remove pan from hot water and set in cold water to cool. Whip egg whites stiff, and whip cream stiff. Combine whites, cream, and vanilla. Beat maple mixture into whites and cream. Pour into chilled tray. Freeze for 1 hour. Turn mixture out into chilled bowl and beat. Pour back into tray and freeze for 3 hours or until thick enough to serve. Serves 8 to 10.

Baked Custard

3 eggs, slightly beaten	¼ cup sugar
¼ tsp. salt	½ tsp. vanilla
2 cups milk, scalded (just before boiling)	nutmeg or cinnamon, garnish

Preheat oven 325°F. Combine eggs, sugar, and salt. Add milk and vanilla slowly. Pour into custard cups. Garnish with nutmeg or cinnamon, optional. Set cups into shallow pan containing about 1 inch hot water. Bake 40 to 45 minutes or until knife inserted in center comes out clean. Serve warm or chilled.

Custard with Meringue Boats

4 cups whole milk	5 egg yolks
½ cup sugar	½ cup flour
dash of salt	1 tsp. each vanilla and almond extracts

Over low heat, combine milk and egg yolks. Mix thoroughly, but do not froth. Heat, but do not boil. Sift together sugar, flour, and salt. Add gradually from sifter into milk and eggs. Continue cooking until mixture thickens; do not boil. When thick, remove from heat and cool to warm. Add extracts and mix well. Cool thoroughly. Top with meringue (see p. 116).

Meringue Boats

5 egg whites   3 tbsp. superfine sugar   dash of salt

Beat room-temperature egg whites until frothy. Add salt and sugar a teaspoon at a time; continue beating until meringue is very stiff. Heat shallow pan with water and gently drop spoonfuls into simmering water. Poach a minute or two on both sides. Let cool on wax paper. Use to top baked custard and garnish with a dusting of cinnamon or chopped nuts.

Old-Fashioned Coconut Custard

4 eggs   ¼ cup brown sugar
1 ½ cups coconut milk (see below)   ¾ cup evaporated milk
½ tsp. cardamom   ¼ tsp. mace
dash of cloves   ¼ tsp. almond extract
shredded coconut for garnish

Beat eggs until whites are no longer stringy, not frothy. Add sugar and coconut milk, stirring until sugar is dissolved. Blend in evaporated milk, spices, and extract. Strain mixture through fine strainer into custard cups. Place cups in baking dish and add boiling water, 1 inch in dish. Bake at 325°F for 1 hour and 15 minutes or until knife comes out clean. Garnish with flaked coconut and serve.

Coconut Milk. Heat 2 ½ cups of whole milk. Add 2 cups flaked or shredded coconut. Simmer for 10 minutes. Pour into blender and use highest speed to mix thoroughly. Pour through cheesecloth to finish.

Peach Cardinale

3 cups water   1 cup sugar
2 large firm, ripe peaches, peeled   1 tbsp. vanilla
raspberry sauce (p. 117)   whipped cream topping (p. 117)

In a large saucepan, combine water and sugar. Bring to a boil for 3 minutes. Reduce heat to low. Add halved peaches and vanilla. Simmer, uncovered, for 10 to 15 minutes or until just tender. Chill peaches in syrup for 1 hour. Make raspberry sauce and whipping cream. Spoon a peach half into serving dish and top with raspberry sauce and whipped cream. Top all with fresh raspberries and serve.

Raspberry Sauce. Mash 10 oz. frozen raspberries, thawed, through a strainer into saucepan. Discard seeds. Mix 1 tbsp. sugar and 2 tsp. cornstarch. Stir in ¼ cup water and add to berry puree. Heat, stirring, to just boiling. Cook until mixture clears and thickens. Chill.

Whipped Cream Topping. Whip ½ cup whipping cream. Add 1 tbsp. powdered sugar and 1 tsp. vanilla, whipping until it holds soft peaks.

Skillet Pudding

1 qt. milk

2/3 cup flour

1 tsp. vanilla

2 eggs, separate yolks and whites

2/3 cup sugar

Blend flour, sugar, yolks, and milk. Shake (like gravy) until blended. Cook until thick. Add vanilla; lightly fold in stiffly beaten egg whites. Take off heat and serve.

*Seven generations ago, after giving birth to her son, our granny was told by the doctor the boy would not live out the week. She fed the baby skillet pudding, and her son lived to carry on the family line. Now we serve this as a dessert in honor of our granny.

Ice Cream

2 ½ cups cream plus 2 cups milk or 4 ½ cups half and half
2 eggs
¼ tsp. salt
1/3 cups brown sugar
3 tbsp. granulated sugar
2 tbsp. vanilla

Beat eggs; add ¼ of milk and all other ingredients. Mix well. Mix in rest of milk. You may add a pint of fresh fruit or 2 or 3 bananas when almost ready. Use ice cream maker. Around maker, put 1 part rock salt to 8 parts of crushed ice.

Old-Fashioned Ice Cream

6 eggs beaten until fluffy
2 tsp. vanilla

2 cups sugar
1 qt. cream

Put eggs, sugar, and vanilla into ice cream maker. If you want fruit, add it now. Fill container with milk to 2 ½ inches from top. Around container, use 1 part rock salt and 8 parts crushed ice.

English Fig Pudding

½ cup butter, room temperature
½ cup molasses
½ tsp. grated lemon peel
½ cup chopped walnuts or pecans
½ tsp. baking soda
1 tsp. salt
¼ tsp. nutmeg

2 eggs
2 cups dried figs, chopped fine
1 cup buttermilk
2 ½ cups flour
2 tsp. baking powder
½ tsp. cinnamon

Preheat oven to 325°F. In a mixer, beat the butter until fluffy. Add eggs and molasses; beat until well blended. Add the figs, lemon peel, buttermilk, and nuts and blend for 1 minute. Sift together the remaining ingredients; add to butter mixture and blend well. Pour into greased and floured 8"× 4" baking dish and bake for about an hour until toothpick comes out clean. Remove from oven and cool slightly. Garnish with whipped cream and serve.

Fudge

3 cups chocolate chips

dash of salt

chopped walnuts, optional

14 oz. sweetened condensed milk

1 ½ tsp. vanilla

Melt chips in double boiler until melted. Remove from heat and add milk, salt, vanilla, and nuts. Pour in baking dish lined with wax paper. Chill.

Almond Roca

1 cup sugar

melted chocolate chips

½ cup butter

¼ cup water

1 tbsp. Karo syrup

½ to ¾ cup chopped nuts

Mix sugar, water, syrup, and butter in heavy skillet. Cook until brown. Be sure to cook long enough. Add nuts when nearly done. Pour into buttered cookie sheet. Cover with melted chocolate chips and smooth out. Chill and cut or break into pieces.

Caramels

1 cup sugar

½ cup butter

½ cup finely chopped nuts

¾ cup dark corn syrup

1 cup light cream

½ tsp. vanilla

Butter sides of heavy 2-quart saucepan and combine sugar, corn syrup, butter, and ½ cup of cream. Bring to a boil over low heat, stirring constantly. Slowly stir in remaining ½ cup cream; cook over low to medium ball stage at 242°F on candy thermometer. Remove from heat; add nuts and vanilla. Pour into buttered 9"× 5"× 3" pan. Mark in 32 squares when partially cool. Cut when cooled. Wrap and store in airtight container.

♥♥♥ Brings back so many memories, sitting around Granny's kitchen table sampling all of her wonderful meals and treats. ♥♥♥

Jell-O Popcorn Balls

6 oz. pkg. Jell-O
1 cup sugar
1 cup Karo light syrup

Cook together all until sugar is dissolved and comes to a good boil. Pour over 6 quarts of cooked popcorn. Butter hands and mix all and shape into balls. Place on wax paper to harden. Wrap in plastic wrap to store.

Disappearing Lollipops

1 pkg. white chocolate chips
12 popsicle sticks
24 red hots

In a saucepan, simmer chips until melted. Line cookie sheet with waxed paper and place sticks about 2 inches apart. Spoon onto stick in shape of a ghost and add red hots for eyes. Chill and wrap in baggies. Great Halloween treat.

Candied Walnuts

1 cup brown sugar, packed	½ cup granulated sugar
½ cup sour cream	dash of salt
1 tsp. vanilla	2 ½ cups walnut halves

Combine brown sugar, granulated sugar, and sour cream in a saucepan. Cook over medium-high heat, stirring until it boils. Continue to boil until mixture reaches soft-ball stage (240°F) or until it forms a soft ball when dropped into cold water. Stir in salt and vanilla. Pour hot candy mixture over walnuts in a mixing bowl and mix until walnuts are evenly coated. Spoon out onto waxed paper. Separate walnuts. Allow to cool and set. When dry, store in airtight container. Makes about 3 cups.

♥ ♥ ♥ Delicious treats the whole family can enjoy. ♥ ♥ ♥

Ginger Bourbon Dessert Sauce

1 cup brown sugar
3 tbsp. butter, unsalted
3 tbsp. bourbon
1/3 cup heavy cream

½ cup maple syrup
dash of salt
1/3 cup preserved ginger, coarsely chopped

In a heavy saucepan, bring to a boil over low heat the sugar, maple syrup, butter, and salt, stirring frequently to dissolve sugar and keep the mixture smooth. Boil for 4 minutes, stirring occasionally. Remove from heat; let cool for 1 minute. Carefully stir in bourbon (mixture may sputter slightly). Fold in the ginger. Add the cream, one tbsp. at a time, stirring well after each addition. Serve the sauce warm. Sauce may be reserved for future use by storing in a jar with a tight lid in the refrigerator. To reheat, pour desired amount onto the top of the double boiler over hot not boiling water. Heat until warm.

Baked Apples

Rome apple
handful of raisins

¼ cup brown sugar
½ tbsp. butter

Carefully remove core of apple and puncture side of apple with a knife for ventilation. Stuff in raisins and brown sugar, top with butter, and place in baking dish at 350°F for 25 to 35 minutes or until apple is soft. Pour Hot Nutmeg Sauce (see below) over baked apple and serve.

Hot Nutmeg Sauce

½ cup sugar   1 tbsp. cornstarch
dash of salt   dash of nutmeg
1 cup boiling water   2 tbsp. butter
1 ½ tbsp. lemon juice

In a saucepan, combine sugar, cornstarch, salt, and nutmeg. Gradually add water. Cook over low heat until thick and clear. Blend in butter and lemon juice. Serve over baked apple. Makes 1 ½ cups of sauce.

Apple Pandowdy

4 cups tart apples, peeled, thinly sliced
¾ cup brown sugar, packed
1 + ¼ cups flour
1 tsp. cinnamon
dash of nutmeg
¾ tsp. salt
1 cup water
2 + 4 tbsp. butter
1 tbsp. lemon juice
2/3 cup milk
2 tsp. baking powder

Arrange apple slices in greased baking dish. In a saucepan, mix brown sugar, ¼ cup flour, the spices, and ¼ tsp. salt. Stir in water. Place over low heat, cook, stirring until thickened. Stir in 2 tbsp. butter and lemon juice and pour over apples. In a bowl, mix remaining flour, salt, and baking powder. Cut in remaining butter until crumbly. With fork, stir in enough milk to make a soft dough. Spoon onto apples, making 8 biscuits. Dust with cinnamon and sugar. Bake at 375°F for 40 minutes or until biscuits are browned and apples are tender.

Brown Betty

6 cups tart apples, peeled, cored, thinly sliced
¾ cup sugar

Place apple slices in baking dish. Sprinkle with sugar.

Topping

1 ¼ cups flour	¾ cup brown sugar, packed
½ tsp. salt	½ cup butter

Combine flour, brown sugar, salt, and butter to crumbly. Crumble over apples and bake at 375°F for 30 to 40 minutes or until top is golden brown and apples are tender.

Cobbler Upside Down

1 ½ cup sugar	¼ cup butter	1 cup flour	1 tsp. baking powder
¼ tsp. salt	½ cup milk	2 cups fruit	1 cup hot fruit juice

Preheat oven to 375°F. Cream ½ cup sugar and butter together. Sift together flour, salt, and baking powder and add to creamed mixture. Mix in milk. Spread in buttered baking dish. In a bowl, mix fruit with 1 cup sugar. Pour in 1 cup hot juice or water. If using apples, add ¾ cup extra juice or water. Cover batter with fruit mixture in baking dish. Bake for 45 minutes.

Peach Cobbler

½ cup butter	½ cup sugar
1 cup flour	¾ cup milk
1 ½ tsp. baking powder	1 ¾ cup peaches
½ cup sugar	1/8 tsp. almond extract
1 tsp. vanilla extract	minute tapioca

Melt butter in baking dish. Mix ½ cup sugar, flour, baking powder, and milk. Pour into (8"× 8") baking dish with melted butter; do not stir. Add peaches on top, and sprinkle with ½ cup sugar and tapioca over peaches. Bake at 350°F for 30 minutes. Double recipe for 9 × 13" baking dish.

Rhubarb Crunch

Crumb Topping

1 cup sifted flour   ¾ cup quick oats
1 cup brown sugar   ½ cup soft butter
1 tsp. cinnamon

Fruit Mixture

4 cups diced rhubarb   1 cup sugar
2 tbsp. cornstarch   1 cup water
1 tsp. vanilla

Mix together crumb topping and press ½ mixture into greased 9"× 9" baking dish. Cover with rhubarb. In a saucepan, combine sugar, cornstarch, water, and vanilla. Cook, stirring until thick and clear. Pour over rhubarb. Top with remaining crumbs. Bake at 350°F for 1 hour or until golden brown. Cut into squares and serve warm.

Cherry Crunch

1 can cherry pie filling 1 tsp. lemon juice   ½ cup butter, soft
1 pkg. butter cake mix   ½ cup chopped nuts

Preheat oven to 350°F. Pour pie filling into 9"× 9" baking dish and spread out. In a bowl, mix lemon juice, butter, cake mix, and nuts until crumbly.

Crumble over cherries and bake for 35 to 45 minutes or until golden brown. Variation: use chocolate cake mix.

Building a Cobbler

Build a cobbler from the bottom up. There are two basic formulas to follow: one for berries and stone fruits (fruits with a center pit, like peaches, apricots, plums, nectarines, and cherries) and one for apples or pears. Follow either recipe and use the fruit of your choice. Stir all ingredients together in 9"× 9" baking dish and set aside to make topping.

Formula for Berries and Stone Fruits

5 ½ cups berries or pitted stone fruits

¼ cup sugar

2 tbsp. quick tapioca

1 tbsp. lemon juice

1 tsp. almond extract

Formula for Apples and Pears

5 cups peeled, cored, sliced apples or pears

1/3 cup sugar

1 tbsp. lemon juice

1 tsp. vanilla

1 tbsp. quick tapioca

1 tbsp. flour

After you have made your filling, you can put two kinds of toppings over it: a crisp and lacy one with oats and a touch of cinnamon or a tender biscuit topping sweetened with brown sugar. Mix and match either topping will work over either fruit mixture. Mix the ingredients in a bowl with a fork, crumble the oat topping, and drop the biscuit topping evenly over the fruit base.

Oat Topping

½ cup flour
½ cup sugar
¼ cup butter
1 tsp. cinnamon

½ cup oats
¼ cup chopped nuts
1 tsp. vanilla
dash of nutmeg

Biscuit Topping

1 cup flour
1/3 cup oats
2 tsp. baking powder
dash of nutmeg

½ cup milk
¼ cup butter
1 tsp. cinnamon

Bake cobbler at 375°F for 30 to 40 minutes or until golden brown.

Peanutty Ice Cream Pie

1 ½ cups coarsely ground peanuts
2 tbsp. sugar
¼ cup corn syrup
3 tbsp. chopped peanuts
chocolate chips and peanut butter chips

3 tbsp. butter, melted
¼ cup flaked coconut
¼ cup peanut butter
qt. vanilla ice cream

Grease 9" pie plate. In a bowl, combine ground peanuts, butter, and sugar. Press mixture firmly onto bottom and sides of pie plate. Chill for 15 minutes in freezer. In a bowl, stir together coconut, corn syrup, peanut butter, and 3 tbsp. chopped peanuts. Place ice cream into large bowl and stir to soften. Stir in the coconut mixture just until combined. Spoon into chilled crust. Sprinkle chocolate and peanut butter chips over pie. Cover, freeze for 6 hours or until firm. Remove from freezer and place the pie on a warm, damp towel for a few minutes before cutting into wedges. Serves 8. Carbs per serving 36 grams.

Chocolate Chip Cheesecake

1 ½ cups graham cracker crumbs	1/3 cup Hershey cocoa
1/3 cup sugar	1/3 cup butter, melted
24 oz. cream cheese, soft	14 oz. sweetened condensed milk
3 eggs	1 tsp. vanilla
1 cup mini chocolate chips	1 tsp. flour

Preheat oven to 300°F. In bowl, combine graham cracker crumbs, cocoa, sugar, and butter and press evenly onto bottom and sides of 9" pie plate. In large bowl, beat cream cheese until fluffy. Gradually add milk, beating until smooth. Add eggs and vanilla; mix well. In a small bowl, toss ½ cup mini chocolate chips with flour to coat. Stir into cheese mixture. Pour into prepared pan. Sprinkle remaining chips evenly over top of pie. Bake for 1 hour, turn oven off, and allow to cool in oven for 1 hour. Remove from oven; cool to room temperature. Refrigerate before serving. Cover and refrigerate leftovers.

Cherry Cheese Torte

1 box yellow cake mix	11 oz. cream cheese, soft
2/3 cup sugar	¼ tsp. nutmeg
2 tbsp. milk	1 large can cherry pie filling

Using 8" or 9" round layer cake pans, make and cool cake as directed on box. Mix soft cream cheese with sugar, nutmeg, and milk; beat until smooth. Split each layer into two thin layers. Spread ½ cup cream cheese mixture and ½ cup cherry pie filling between each layer and on top of cake. Keep refrigerated.

Sour Cream Apple Coffee Cake

1 cup butter, soft	2 ¼ cups sugar
4 eggs	2 ½ cups flour
½ tsp. salt	½ tsp. baking powder
½ tsp. baking soda	1 cup sour cream
1 tsp. vanilla	3 cups chopped apples
¼ cup brown sugar, packed	½ tsp. cinnamon
1 cup nuts	

Preheat oven to 350°F. Generously grease and flour heavy Bundt pan or 10" tube pan. In a large bowl, cream the butter with 2 cups of the sugar until light and fluffy. Beat in eggs. Stir together the flour, salt, baking powder, and baking soda. Beat the flour mixture into the butter mixture alternately with the sour cream. Beat in the vanilla. Peel and chop apples and mix with the remaining ¼ cup sugar; fold into the batter.

Spoon half of the batter into the prepared Bundt pan. Smooth with a spatula. In a medium bowl, combine the brown sugar and cinnamon, and stir in the chopped nuts. Sprinkle the nut mixture over the batter in the pan. Top with the remaining batter and smooth with a spatula.

Bake for 70 minutes or until toothpick inserted comes out clean. Turn onto a rack to cool before serving.

Triple Fudge Cake

1 pkg. chocolate pudding mix (not instant)	½ cup chocolate chips
1 pkg. sour cream chocolate cake mix	½ cup chopped nuts

Preheat oven to 350°F. Grease and flour 9"× 13" baking pan. In a large saucepan, cook pudding as directed on box. Blend dry cake mix into hot pudding; beat by hand for about 2 minutes. Pour into pan and sprinkle with chocolate chips and nuts. Bake for 30 to 35 minutes. Top with whipped cream.

Carrot Cake

1 ½ cups brown sugar, packed	¾ cup olive oil
4 eggs	1 tsp. salt
½ tsp. cinnamon	½ tsp. allspice
1 ½ cups flour	2 ½ cups shredded carrot
1 ½ cups oats	½ cup raisins
1 tbsp. baking powder	¾ cup chopped nuts

Preheat oven to 350°F. Grease and flour 9"× 13" baking pan. In a large bowl, combine sugar and oil; next add eggs one at a time, beating well after each addition. In a medium bowl, combine remaining ingredients. Add sugar mixture, mixing just until dry ingredients are moistened. Pour into pan. Bake 45 to 50 minutes or until toothpick comes out clean. Cool for 10 minutes; remove from pan. Cool completely on wire rack and drizzle with butter frosting (see below).

Golden Butter Frosting

½ cup butter	2 cups sifted powdered sugar
1 tsp. vanilla	

Melt butter until just golden brown. Blend in powdered sugar and the vanilla. If necessary, add 1 to 6 drops of water until right consistency, more for drizzling, less for spreading over cake or cookies.

Boysenberry Gingerbread with Sauce

1/3 cup butter
½ cup brown sugar, packed
1 egg, beaten
¾ cup molasses
2 cups flour
1 tsp. each baking powder and soda

2 tsp. ginger

1 tsp. cinnamon

¾ cup warm water

1 ¼ cups frozen boysenberries, unthawed, tossed in 1 tbsp. flour

Gingerbread. Cream butter and sugar. Beat in egg, followed by molasses. In a bowl, combine flour, baking powder, baking soda, ginger, and cinnamon. Add dry ingredients alternately with the water, stirring only until moistened. Do not overbeat. Gently fold in berries. Pour into a 9"× 9" baking dish. Bake at 350°F for 50 minutes or until center springs back. Serve with pudding sauce.

Pudding Sauce. In a double boiler, heat ¼ cup sugar, 3 tbsp. butter, ½ tsp. vanilla, and 3 tbsp. half and half.

Old-Fashioned Butter Cake

1 cup butter	2 cups sugar	1 tsp. vanilla
4 eggs	3 cups flour	1 tsp. baking soda
1 tsp. salt	1 cup buttermilk	sifted powdered sugar

Beat together butter and sugar until fluffy. Beat in vanilla. Add eggs one at a time, blending well after each addition. Combine flour with baking soda and salt. Add to batter alternately with buttermilk, beginning and ending with flour. Butter and flour baking dish and pour in batter.

Bake at 250°F for about 1 ½ hours or until a toothpick inserted comes out clean. Allow cake to stand for 5 minutes and remove from pan and finish cooling on a rack. Dust with powdered sugar before serving.

Berry Dream Cake

1 pkg. white cake mix	½ cup water
1 pkg. berry Jell-O mix	5 oz. frozen berries, thawed
2 tbsp. flour	¾ cup cooking oil
4 eggs	Dream Whip

Mix cake mix, Jell-O, flour, eggs, and water. Beat for 2 minutes. Add berries and beat for 1 minute. Add oil and beat for 1 minute. Pour into two greased and floured 9" cake pans.

Bake at 350°F for 35 minutes. Frost with Dream Whip. May be topped with additional berries.

Lemon Supreme Pound Cake

1 pkg. Lemon Cake Mix	1 pkg. lemon instant pudding mix
½ cup cooking oil	1 cup water
4 eggs	

Blend all ingredients in a large bowl. Beat for 2 minutes.
Bake in greased and floured baking pans at 350°F for 45 to 55 minutes until center springs back when touched. Cool right side up for 25 minutes then remove from pan. Glaze (see below) and serve.

Glaze

1 cup powdered sugar	2 tbsp. lemon juice or milk

Mix and drizzle over cake.

♥ Sweet memories of the wonderful aromas from
Granny's kitchen. ♥

Wacky Cake

Preheat oven to 350°F. Sift the following into an ungreased 9"× 13" cake pan that you will bake cake in.

3 cups flour	2 tsp. soda
1 tsp. salt	2 cups sugar
3 tbsp. cocoa	

Add the following:

¾ cup cooking oil	1 tsp. vanilla
2 tbsp. vinegar	2 cups cold water

Mix with fork. Do NOT BEAT! Bake for 25 to 30 minutes. Cool and frost (see below) and serve.

White Frosting

Cream ½ cup butter until soft. Add 1/8 tsp. salt. Blend in part of 1 pound (about 4 ½ cups) confectioner's sugar. Blend in 1 tsp. vanilla. Add remaining sugar alternately with about 4 tbsp. milk, beating until smooth. Makes 1 ¾ cups frosting.

Bacardi Rum Cake

1 cup chopped walnuts	1 pkg. yellow cake mix
1 pkg. Jell-O vanilla instant pudding	4 eggs
½ cup cold water	½ cup veggie oil
½ cup Bacardi dark rum (80 proof)	

Sprinkle nut in bottom of greased and floured Bundt pan. Combine cake, pudding, eggs, water, oil, and rum in large bowl. Blend then beat for 2 minutes. Pour into pan. Bake at 325°F for 60 minutes or until cake springs back. Cool for 15 minutes.

Glaze. Combine 1 cup sugar, ½ cup butter, and ¼ cup water in a saucepan. Bring to a boil for 5 minutes, stirring continually. Remove from heat. Stir in ½ cup Bacardi dark rum and just bring to boil. Remove cake from pan onto plate and spoon warm glaze over cake.

Funnel Cakes

1 egg, beaten	2/3 cup milk
1 tsp. baking powder	1 ¼ cups flour
2 tbsp. sugar	¼ tsp. salt
powdered sugar for topping	oil for frying

Mix egg and milk. Sift dry ingredients and gradually add to milk mixture. Beat until smooth. Preheat oil in frying pan to 375°F. Pour batter into hot oil with a funnel with a ½" or ¾" hole. Let batter drizzle into hot oil, spiraling to create a circle. Cook for about 1 minute; flip over, cooking both sides. Remove and drain on paper towels. Sprinkle with powdered sugar and top with fruit preserves while still warm

Pineapple Upside Down Cake

Duncan Hines Pineapple Supreme Deluxe Cake Mix
½ cup butter
1 cup brown sugar
1 lb. 14 oz. can pineapple slices
whipped cream

Melt butter in 9"× 13" baking dish. Sprinkle brown sugar in bottom of pan. Drain pineapple and save the syrup. Arrange pineapple in the sugar mixture. Add enough water to pineapple syrup to make 1 1/3 cup liquid and add this and 2 eggs to the cake mix and mix according to package. Pour batter over fruit. Bake at 350°F for 50 minutes or until cake pulls away from the sides of pan. Let stand for 5 minutes for topping to begin to set. Then turn upside down onto large platter or cookie sheet. Serve pieces of cake topped with whipped cream.

"Bring a little sunshine to your table by baking your favorite treat."

Lazy Daisy Cake

2 eggs	1 cup sugar	1 tsp. vanilla
1 cup flour	1 tsp. baking powder	½ tsp. salt
½ cup milk	1 tbsp. butter (hard)	

Beat eggs until frothy. Add sugar 2 tbsp. at a time while beating until thickened. Add vanilla and beat well. Combine flour, baking powder, and salt in a small bowl. Add to egg mixture and stir. Heat and stir milk and butter in a saucepan on medium heat until butter is melted. Add to flour mixture and mix well. Spread batter in greased 9" square baking dish and bake at 350°F for 25 to 30 minutes until toothpick comes out clean. Top with Coconut Topping (see below) and serve.

Coconut Frosting

3 tbsp. hard butter
½ cup brown sugar, packed
2 tbsp. half and half cream or butter milk
½ coconut, flaked

Cream butter, brown sugar, and cream into saucepan and bring to a rolling boil over medium-high heat, stirring occasionally. Remove from heat. Add coconut and stir. Spread over warm cake. Return to oven for about 3 minutes at 350°F until topping is bubbling. Let stand in pan on wire rack until cool.

"The way to a man's heart is through his stomach."

Sour Cream Gingerbread

1 ¾ cups flour

1 ¼ tsp. baking soda

½ tsp. salt

1/3 cup butter

2/3 cup sour cream

powdered sugar

1 ¾ tsp. ground ginger

½ tsp. ground cloves

2/3 cup dark molasses

¼ cup maple syrup

1 egg, beaten until foamy

Preheat oven to 350°F. Butter and flour 9" square baking dish. Sift together the flour, ginger, baking soda, cloves, and salt into large bowl. In a small saucepan, stir together over low heat the molasses, butter, and maple syrup until boiling point. Remove from heat and cool. Make a well in the flour mixture and add butter mixture and sour cream. Stir just until well blended. Stir in egg. Pour batter into prepared pan and bake for 25 to 30 minutes or until stick comes out clean. Let cool on wire rack for about 10 minutes. Loosen edges with a knife and remove from pan. Sprinkle top with powdered sugar and serve warm.

Applesauce Spice Cake

Sift together the following:

2 cups flour	1 ½ cups sugar	2 ½ tsp. baking powder
1 tsp. salt	1 tsp. cinnamon	½ tsp. nutmeg
¼ tsp. cloves		

Add the following:

½ cup canola oil

1 tsp. vanilla

2/3 cup applesauce

1 cup grated or finely chopped apples, peeled and cored

Beat for 2 minutes then add 1/3 cup milk and 2 eggs, then beat for 2 minutes. Bake at 350°F for 30 to 35 minutes for layers or 40 to 45 minutes for oblong baking dish. Frost (see below) and serve.

Penuche Icing

Melt ½ cup butter in a saucepan and add 1 cup brown sugar, packed to a boil over low heat for 2 minutes. Stir constantly. Stir in ¼ cup milk, bring to boil, stir constantly. Remove from heat. Cool to lukewarm. Gradually add 1 ¾ cup powdered sugar. Beat until thick enough to spread.

Even Dozen Cinnamon Rolls

½ pkg. active dry yeast	1 ¾ cup sifted flour
½ + 1/8 cup milk	1/8 cup sugar
1/8 cup butter	½ tsp. salt
1 egg	

Combine 1 cup flour and yeast. Heat milk, sugar, butter, salt just until warm. Add to dry ingredients; next add egg and beat while scraping bowl. Beat 3 minutes. Stir in ¾ cup flour. Place in greased bowl. Turn onto grease surface. Cover and let rise for 1 ½ to 2 hours. Next roll out on lightly floured surface to 16"× 8" rectangle. Melt together ½ cup sugar, 2 tbsp. melted butter, and 1 tsp. cinnamon and spread over rolled-out dough. Roll up and seal edges and cut into 12 sections. Next place on 9"× 9" greased baking dish. Cover and let rise for 45 minutes. Bake at 375°F until done. Top with glaze (see below) and serve. Makes 12.

Glaze

1 cup powdered sugar	2 tbsp. milk
½ tsp. vanilla	dash of salt

Blend and drizzle over top of cinnamon rolls.

Chewy Blond Brownies

1 ¼ cups brown sugar, packed   ½ cup chopped nuts

2/3 cup butter   2 eggs

1 1/3 cups Quaker Oats   2 tsp. vanilla

1 1/3 cups flour   ¾ tsp. each salt and soda

½ cup white chocolate, butterscotch, or peanut butter chips

Preheat oven to 350°F. Grease 9"× 13" baking dish. In a bowl, combine sugar and butter until smooth. Add remaining ingredients and mix well. Spread into pan and bake for 25 minutes or until golden brown. Cool and cut into bars.

Grand Cinnamon Rolls

1 cup warm water   2 pkg. active dry yeast

1 cup warm milk   1 tsp. + 2/3 + 1 ½ + ¼ cup granulated sugar

2 tsp. salt   2/3 + ½ + ½ + 2/3 cups butter, melted

2 eggs, slightly beaten   8 cups flour

3 tbsp. cinnamon   4 cups powdered sugar

2 tsp. vanilla   6 tbsp. hot water

walnuts

In a small bowl, mix together warm water, yeast, and 1 tsp. sugar and set aside. In a large bowl, mix milk, 2/3 cup sugar, 2/3 cup melted butter, salt, and eggs. Stir well and add to yeast mixture. Add half the flour and beat until smooth. Stir in enough of the remaining flour until dough is slightly stiff (dough will be sticky). Turn onto well-floured board and knead 5 to 10 minutes. Place in well-buttered bowl, cover, and let rise in warm place free from drafts until double in size, for about 1 to 1 ½ hours.

When doubled, punch down dough and let rest for 5 minutes. Roll onto floured surface into a 15"× 20" rectangle. Spread dough with ½ cup melted butter. Mix together 1 ½ cups sugar and cinnamon then sprinkle over buttered dough. Sprinkle with walnuts, and roll up jellyroll fashion and pinch edge together to seal. Cut into 12 to 15 slices. Coat bottom of 9"× 13" and 8" square baking pans with ½ cup melted butter then sprinkle with ¼ cup sugar. Place cinnamon roll slices close together in pans. Let rise in warm place until dough is doubled in size for about 45 minutes.

Bake in preheated oven at 350°F for 25 to 30 minutes or until rolls are nicely browned. Cool rolls slightly.

Meanwhile, in medium bowl, mix melted butter, powdered sugar, and vanilla. Add hot water 1 tbsp. at a time until glaze reaches desired spreading consistency. Spread over slightly cooled rolls and serve warm.
Makes 12 to 15 large cinnamon rolls.

Brownies

Bring to boil the following:

1 cup butter	1 cup water	2 tbsp. cocoa

Remove from heat. While this cools, mix in a bowl the following:

2 cups sugar	1 tsp. soda	2 cups flour
½ cup buttermilk	½ tsp. salt	1 tsp. vanilla
2 eggs		

Pour onto greased and floured 11"× 17" cookie sheet and bake at 350°F for 20 minutes. Frost while warm and serve.

Frosting

Bring to a boil the following:

½ cup butter   3 tbsp. cocoa   6 tbsp. buttermilk

Remove from heat and add 1 tsp. vanilla and powdered sugar to right
consistency then add ½ cup walnuts. Frost brownies while still warm.

Peanut Butter and Jam Bars

½ cup sugar   ½ cup brown sugar, packed
½ cup butter   ½ cup peanut butter
1 egg   1 ¼ cups flour
¾ tsp. baking soda   ¼ tsp. baking powder
½ cup jam

Preheat oven to 350°F. Mix sugars, butters, and egg. Stir in flour, baking
soda, and baking powder. Set aside 1 cup dough. Press remaining dough in
ungreased 9"× 13" baking dish and spread with your favorite jam. Crumble
last of dough over jam and bake until golden brown for about 20 minutes.
Cool and drizzle with glaze (see below). Cut into bars and serve.

Glaze

2 tbsp. butter   1 tsp. vanilla
1 cup powdered sugar   1 to 2 tbsp. hot water

In a saucepan, heat butter until melted. Mix in powdered sugar and vanilla.
Beat in hot water 1 tsp. at a time until smooth and right consistency.

Coconut Fudge Peanut Butter Bars

1 pkg. yellow cake mix   1 cup peanut butter

2 eggs   ½ cup butter, soft

In a large bowl, combine cake mix, peanut butter, butter, and eggs and mix well. Press by hand 2/3 dough into bottom of ungreased 9"× 13" baking dish. Prepare filling (below) and spread over dough. Crumble rest of dough on top, and bake at 350°F for 20 to 25 minutes. Cool and cut into bars.

Filling

1 cup chocolate chips   14 oz. sweetened condensed milk

2 tbsp. butter   1 pkg. coconut pecan or almond frosting mix

In a saucepan, combine chocolate chips, milk, and butter and melt over low heat. Stir until smooth. Remove from heat and stir in frosting mix.

Dream Bars

½ cup butter   ½ cup brown sugar, packed   1 cup flour

Preheat oven to 350°F. Mix butter and sugar until creamy and stir in flour. Press by hand into 9"× 13" baking dish, and bake for 10 minutes. Spread with topping (below) and return to oven and bake for an additional 25 minutes or until golden brown. Cool then cut into bars.

Topping

2 eggs, well beaten   1 cup brown sugar   1 tsp. vanilla

2 tbsp. flour   1 tsp. baking powder   ½ tsp. salt

1 cup coconut   1 cup chopped nuts   1 cup chocolate chips

Mix together flour, baking powder, and salt. Set aside. Mix well beaten eggs, sugar, and vanilla; blend into flour mixture. Stir in coconut, nuts, and chocolate chips.

Ginger Cream Cookies

½ cup sugar	1/3 cup butter	1 egg
½ cup molasses	½ cup water	2 cups flour
1 tsp. ginger	½ tsp. baking soda	½ tsp. nutmeg
½ tsp. cloves	½ tsp. cinnamon	½ tsp. salt

Mix sugar, butter, egg, molasses, and water. Stir in remaining ingredients. Cover and refrigerate for at least 1 hour.

Preheat oven to 400°F. Drop dough by spoon about 2 inches apart onto ungreased cookie sheet. Bake until almost no indentation remains when touched for about 8 minutes. Remove immediately from cookie sheet and cool. Frost with vanilla butter frosting (see below). Makes 4 dozen cookies.

Vanilla Butter Frosting

½ cup butter	2 cups powdered sugar
1 tsp. vanilla	1 tsp. milk

Mix butter and powdered sugar until creamy. Beat in vanilla and milk until smooth and of spreading consistency.

Granny's Date Cookies

1 cup butter	2 cups sugar
3 eggs	1 tbsp. cream
2 tsp. cinnamon	1 tsp. cloves
1 tsp. nutmeg	1 tsp. vanilla
1 cup finely chopped dates	4 cups flour
1 tsp. baking soda	½ tsp. salt
walnut halves	

Cream butter and sugar. Add rest of the ingredients and mix well. Chill for 2 hours or longer.

Break bits of dough and flatten down with glass 3 inches apart on greased baking sheet. Flatten with knife that has been dipped in cold water. Put walnut half on top of cookie and bake for 10 minutes in 350°F (moderate heat).

Walnut Raisin Bars

1 + 2/3 cups sugar	2/3 cup butter
1 + 1 tsp. vanilla	1 + 3 eggs
2 cups flour	½ cup corn syrup
¼ cup molasses	1 cup broken walnuts or pecans
1 cup raisins	

Preheat oven to 350°F. Mix 1 cup sugar, butter, 1 tsp. vanilla, and 1 egg. Stir in flour. Press dough in ungreased 9"× 13" baking dish. Bake until edges are light brown for about 15 minutes. Beat 3 eggs, 2/3 cup sugar, corn syrup, molasses, and 1 tsp. vanilla. Stir in nuts and raisins, and pour over crust. Bake until set for about 25 to 30 minutes. Cool completely, loosen edges from sides of pan, and cut into bars.

Crunchy Surprise Bars

1 cup sugar	1 cup butter
¼ cup molasses	1 egg yolk
1 tsp. vanilla	2 cups flour
12 oz. chocolate chips	1 cup peanuts
1 cup seedless raisins	1/3 cup peanut butter

Preheat oven to 350°F. Cream sugar, butter, molasses, egg yolk, and vanilla. Stir in flour and 1 cup chocolate chips. Press dough in ungreased 9"× 13" baking dish. Bake until golden brown for 25 to 30 minutes. Mix remaining chips, raisins, peanuts, and peanut butter in a saucepan. Heat over medium-low heat, stirring constantly, until chocolate is melted. Spread over crust in pan. Refrigerate for at least 2 hours. Cut into bars.

Shortbread

2 cups flour
½ cup powdered sugar
1 cup butter

Combine flour and sugar. Cut in butter, should be crumbly. Press into ungreased 9"× 9" baking dish. Prick entire dough with fork. Bake at 300°F for 50 to 60 minutes or until golden. Cool on rack and cut into squares.

Chocolate Peanut Rice Krispies Treats

1 cup smooth peanut butter
1 cup chocolate chips
1 cup salted peanuts

¾ cup liquid honey
3 cups Rice Krispies cereal

Heat peanut butter and honey in a saucepan on low heat, stirring often until melted. Bring to a gentle boil and remove from heat. Add chocolate chips; stir until smooth. Remove from heat. Add cereal and peanuts. Stir until coated. Press firmly in wax paper–lined 9"× 9" baking dish. Chill until firm and cut into squares.

Matrimonial Squares

Crumb Layers

1 ½ cups rolled oats
1 cup brown sugar, packed
½ tsp. salt

1 ¼ cups flour
1 tsp. baking soda
1 cup butter

Combine oats, flour, brown sugar, soda, and salt in a bowl. Cut in butter until crumbly. Press a little more than half into greased 9"× 9" baking dish. Set aside remainder.

Date Filling

1 ½ cups pitted dates, chopped
2/3 cup water
½ cup sugar

Preheat oven to 350°F. Combine dates, water, and sugar in a saucepan and bring to boil with medium heat. Reduce heat and simmer, uncovered, for about 10 minutes until dates are softened and water is almost evaporated, adding more water if necessary while simmering to soften dates. Spread over layer of crumbs. Sprinkle remaining crumb mixture over top. Press down lightly.

Bake for about 30 minutes or until golden brown. Let cool on rack and cut into squares.

Cherry Squares

Bottom Layer

1 ¼ cup flour
1/3 cup brown sugar, packed
½ cup butter

Combine flour and brown sugar in bowl. Cut in butter until crumbly. Press firmly in ungreased 9"× 9" baking dish.

Bake at 350°F for 15 minutes. Remove from oven.

Second Layer

2 eggs	1 ¼ cups brown sugar, packed
1 tbsp. flour	½ tsp. baking powder
1/8 tsp. salt	1 cup coconut
½ cup chopped walnuts	½ cup chopped cherries

Beat eggs until frothy. Add remaining ingredients in order given, stirring after each addition. Spread evenly over bottom layer.

Bake for 25 minutes or until golden. Cool on rack completely.

Vanilla Icing

2 cups powdered sugar	¼ cup butter
2 tbsp. milk or water	1 tsp. vanilla

Beat all ingredients until smooth, adding more milk or sugar as necessary until of spreading consistency. Spread over second layer. Cut into bars.

Lemon Balls

lemon cake mix
½ cup butter
1 tbsp. water
1 ½ cups Rice Krispies cereal
1 egg, slightly beaten

Mix together in a large bowl. Roll into balls. Bake at 350°F for 10 to 12 minutes. Makes 6 dozen.

M&M Cookies

1 cup butter	½ cup sugar
1 cup brown sugar, packed	1 tsp. vanilla
2 eggs	2 ¼ cups flour
1 tsp. baking soda	1 tsp. salt
1 ½ cups M&Ms	

Preheat oven to 375°F. Blend butter and sugars. Beat in vanilla and eggs. Sift dry ingredients together and add to the sugar mixture. Stir in M&Ms, saving some to top cookies. Drop by teaspoon onto ungreased cookie sheet. Top cookies with M&Ms, and bake for 10 to 12 minutes.

Richest Bars Around

1 stick butter	1 ½ cups graham crack crumbs
12 oz. butterscotch chips	12 oz. chocolate chips
coconut	chopped nuts
14 oz. sweetened condensed milk	

Preheat oven to 350°F. Melt butter and mix with crumbs. Press into 9"× 13" baking dish. Layer butterscotch chips, next chocolate chips. Cover with coconut and chopped nuts. Pour sweetened condensed milk over top and bake for 20 to 30 minutes. Cut into bars.

Reese's Peanut Butter Cup Look-A-likes

1 cup butter	1 lb. powdered sugar
1 ½ cups peanut butter	1 ½ cup graham cracker crumbs
12 oz. chocolate chips	

Cream soft butter with peanut butter. Mix in powdered sugar. Blend well. Add graham cracker crumbs. Press into ungreased 9"× 13" baking dish or cookie sheet. Melt chips and pour over mixture like frosting. Put in refrigerator to firm up; remove 20 minutes before cutting into squares. Keep refrigerated until ready to serve if you want chocolate to be firm.

Lemon Crunch Bars

Bottom Layer

1 1/3 cups soda cracker crumbs	¾ cup butter
¾ cup flour	½ cup sugar
½ cup coconut	1 tsp. baking powder

Combine all ingredients until crumbly. Reserve 1 cup for topping. Press remainder into 9"× 9" baking dish. Bake at 350°F for 15 minutes. Remove from oven.

Lemon Filling

3 eggs
1 cup sugar
lemon, grated peel and juice from 1 lemon
¼ cup butter

Beat eggs in a saucepan and add rest of the ingredients. Heat and stir on medium heat until thickened. Spread over crumb layer in pan. Sprinkle reserved crumb mixture over top and bake for 20 more minutes until golden brown. Let cool on rack then cut into squares.

Noodle Crunch Cookies

1 cup chocolate chips	1 cup butterscotch chips
¼ cup butter	¼ cup smooth peanut butter
2 cups chow mien noodles	1 cup peanuts

Heat chips and butters in a saucepan on low heat, stirring often until chips are almost melted. Do NOT overheat. Remove from heat. Stir until smooth.

Add noodles and peanuts. Stir until coated. Mixture will be soft. Drop using 2 teaspoons for each onto wax paper–lined cookie sheets. Let cool until set. May be chilled in fridge.

Granny's Best Cookie

1 cup sugar
1 cup peanut butter
1 egg
chocolate stars

Mix sugar, peanut butter, and egg well and roll into balls. Press chocolate star onto each ball. Bake at 350°F for 8 to 10 minutes. May substitute chocolate kisses for stars.

Snickerdoodles

1 cup butter, soft	1 ½ cup sugar	2 eggs
2 tsp. vanilla	2 ¾ cups flour, sifted	2 tsp. cream of tartar
1 tsp. baking soda	½ tsp. salt	

Cream butter, sugar, and eggs and chill for 1 hour. Shape into balls and roll into mixture of 2 tbsp. cinnamon and ½ cup sugar. Bake at 400°F for 8 to 10 minutes.

Tea Cookies

1 cup butter, soft	½ cup sugar	½ cup brown sugar
1 egg	1 tsp. vanilla	2 ½ cups flour
1 tsp. baking soda	1 tsp. cream of tartar	½ tsp. salt
½ cup chopped nuts	sugar for dipping	

Preheat oven to 350°F. Grease baking sheet. Cream butter and sugar together until smooth. Beat in egg and vanilla. Mix thoroughly. Sift together flour, baking soda, cream of tartar, and salt. Add to mixture and mix well. Stir in nuts. Chill dough until easy to handle.

Shape into balls. Dip tops in sugar and arrange on prepared baking sheets. Sprinkle several drops of water on each cookie. Bake for 15 minutes or until golden brown.

Chocolate Mounds

chocolate cake mix	½ cup butter
1 ½ cups Rice Krispies cereal	3 tbsp. water
1 egg, slightly whipped	12 oz. chocolate chips

Preheat oven to 350 degrees. Mix and roll into balls. Bake on ungreased cookie sheet for 10 to 12 minutes. Makes 6 dozen.

Cocoa Mound Cookies

3 cups coconut	½ cup butter
2 cups powder sugar	3 squares semisweet chocolate, melted

Melt butter and add powdered sugar and coconut. Shape into balls. Indent balls and pour in melted chocolate on top of each ball.

Brownie Mounds

3 ½ cups sifted flour	1 tsp. baking powder
½ tsp. salt	2/3 cup butter
1 ½ cups sugar	2/3 cup karo syrup
2 eggs	6 oz. unsweetened chocolate squares
2 tsp. vanilla	1 ½ cups chopped nuts

Preheat oven to 350°F. Grease cookie sheet. Melt chocolate over low heat, stirring constantly; set aside. Sift together flour, baking powder, and salt.

Mix butter and sugar until creamy. Stir in Karo corn syrup and eggs. Stir in flour mixture, melted chocolate, vanilla, and chopped nuts. Drop onto prepared cookie sheet. Bake for 10 minutes. Makes over 8 dozen.

Sugar Roll-Out Cookies

1 cup butter	2 cups sugar
1 ½ tsp. vanilla	2 eggs
3 ½ cups flour	4 tsp. baking powder
1 tsp. salt	

Cream together butter, sugar, and vanilla. Add rest of the ingredients and mix well. Roll out dough onto floured surface and cut and bake on greased cookie sheet at 400°F for 5 to 10 minutes.

Blarney Stone Cookies

2 cups powdered sugar
1 cup butter, soft
1 egg
1 ½ tsp. vanilla
2 ¼ cups flour
2 egg yolks
2 tbsp. water
1 ½ cups finely chopped dry roasted peanuts

Preheat oven to 350°F. Combine powdered sugar, butter, egg, and vanilla in bowl. Beat, scraping bowl often, until light and fluffy (about 2 to 3 minutes). Shape into 1-inch balls (use a teaspoon for measuring). Mix well egg yolks and water with a fork. Dip balls of dough into egg mixture and then into peanuts.

Place on ungreased cookie sheet. Bake for 12 to 16 minutes or until top springs back. Makes about 4 dozen cookies. An excellent Butter Cookies.

Coconut Macaroons

2 cups flaked coconut	½ cup sliced almonds
½ cup flour	¼ tsp. salt
4 egg whites	½ tsp. almond extract
½ cup sugar	

Preheat oven to 325°F. Butter cookie sheet.

Combine coconut, almonds, flour, salt; set aside. Beat egg whites until frothy. Add sugar, 1 tablespoon at a time while beating, until soft peaks form. Fold coconut mixture into egg white mixture until just moistened.

Drop using 2 tablespoons for each, about 2 inches apart, onto prepared cookie sheet. Bake for 15 minutes until edges are golden. Let stand on cookie sheets for 5 minutes before removing. Makes about 30 macaroons.

Granny's Famous Oatmeal Cookies

1 cup butter	1 cup brown sugar, packed
½ cup sugar	2 eggs
1 tsp. cinnamon	1 tsp. vanilla
1 ½ cups flour	½ tsp. salt
1 tsp. soda	3 cups oats

Beat butter, sugars, eggs, water, and vanilla together until creamy. Sift together flour, salt, soda, and cinnamon and add to creamy mixture. Blend well. Stir in oats, and drop onto greased cookie sheet. Bake at 350°F for 12 to 15 minutes. Makes 5 dozen. For variations, add 1 cup of nuts, chocolate, or peanut butter or butterscotch chips, raisins, or coconut.

Old-Fashioned Peanut Butter Cookies

Mix together the following:

1 cup butter	1 cup sugar
1 cup brown sugar, packed	2 eggs
1 tsp. vanilla	

Stir in the following:

1 cup peanut butter	3 cups sifted flour
2 tsp. soda	½ tsp. salt

Drop onto ungreased cookie sheet. Press with fork. Bake at 350°F for 10 minutes. Makes 5 dozen.

Chocolate Chip Cookies

1 cup brown sugar	1 cup sugar	3 sticks butter, soft
2 tsp. vanilla	3 eggs, beaten	5 cups flour, sifted
1 1/2 tsp. soda	1 tsp. salt	1 cup nuts, chopped
4 cups chocolate chips		

Preheat oven to 375° F. Cream together butter and sugars. Beat in vanilla then eggs. Sift flour, soda, salt, and beat into creamed mixture. Stir in nuts and chocolate chips. Drop by small cookie scoop onto baking sheet and bake for 8 to 10 minutes. Makes 5 dozen cookies.

Oatmeal Scotchies

1 cup butter	2 cups brown sugar, packed
2 eggs	1 tsp. vanilla
2 cups flour	1 tsp. baking powder

½ tsp. baking soda

2 cups butterscotch chips

2 cups rolled oats

¾ cup unsweetened coconut

Beat butter and sugar until creamy. Add eggs, one at a time, beating after each addition. Beat in vanilla. Combine flour, baking powder, soda, and add to butter mixture. Mix well. Add oats, chips, coconut, and stir until well distributed. Drop onto greased cookie sheet about 2 inches apart.

Bake at 350°F for 8 to 10 minutes until golden brown. Let stand on cookie sheet for 5 minutes before removing. Makes about 5 dozen.

Swedish Tea Cakes

½ cup butter, soft

1 egg yolk

½ tsp. baking powder

1 egg

jam or jelly, your favorite (red is best)

¼ cup brown sugar, packed

1 cup flour

1/8 tsp. salt

2/3 cup nuts, chopped finely

Cream butter and brown sugar together; then add egg yolk and beat well. Combine flour, baking powder, and salt. Add to butter mixture. Stir until stiff dough forms. Roll dough into balls. Dip balls into egg white and roll in nuts. Arrange balls about 2 inches apart on greased cookie sheet. Dent each with thumb and bake at 325°F for 5 minutes.

Remove from oven. Press dents again and bake for 10 to 15 more minutes until golden brown. Let stand on cookie sheet for 5 minutes before removing to wire rack. Fill each dent with 1 tsp. jam or jelly. (Unfilled tea cakes may be stored in airtight container and filling added just before serving.) Makes about 20 tea cakes.

Date Nut Cookies

¾ cup sugar

½ cup baking powder

1 lb. chopped dates

¼ tsp. vanilla

½ cup flour

¼ tsp. salt

2 cups nuts, walnuts or pecans or almonds

3 egg whites, stiffly beaten

Preheat oven to 325°F. Grease cookie sheet. Combine dry ingredients and mix with dates, nuts, and vanilla. Mix in egg whites. Drop by teaspoon onto prepared cookie sheet. Bake for 15 minutes.

Butterscotch Crunches

3 tbsp. smooth peanut butter

3 cups cornflakes cereal

1 cup butterscotch chips

½ cup chopped walnuts

Heat peanut butter and chips in a saucepan on low heat, stirring often, until chips are almost melted. Do NOT OVERHEAT. Remove from heat. Stir until smooth. Add cereal and nuts. Stir until coated. Drop onto waxed paper and cool until set. Makes about 30 cookies.

Toffee Crunch

35 saltine crackers

1/3 cup butter

½ cup brown sugar

6 squares semisweet baking chocolate, chopped

½ cup walnuts, chopped

Preheat oven to 400°F. Line cookie sheet with foil. Spread crackers evenly on foil. Place butter and sugar in a saucepan and bring to a boil on medium-high heat, stirring frequently. Reduce to low and boil for 3 minutes. Do NOT STIR. Immediately spread over crackers.

Bake for 7 minutes. Immediately sprinkle with chocolate. Let stand for 5 minutes. Spread melted chocolate over tops of crackers. Sprinkle with nuts. Cool and break into pieces.

Pumpkin Spice Roll

3/4 cup plus 2 tbsp. powdered sugar, divided
¾ cup flour
1 ½ tsp. pumpkin pie spice
1 tsp. baking powder
¼ tsp. salt
3 eggs
1 cup sugar
¾ cup canned pumpkin
1 cup chopped walnuts
4 oz. cream cheese, soft
1 ½ cups Cool Whip or french vanilla whipped topping

Preheat oven to 375°F. Grease a cookie sheet and line it with wax paper; grease and flour paper also. Sprinkle clean towel with ¼ cup powdered sugar. Mix flour, spice, baking powder, and salt; set aside. Beat eggs and sugar in bowl until thick. Add pumpkin and mix well. Add flour mixture; beat just until blended. Spread evenly into prepared pan; sprinkle with walnuts. Bake for 15 minutes or until top of cake springs back. Immediately invert cake onto towel and remove pan. Carefully peel off paper. Starting at one of the short sides, roll up cake and towel together. Cool completely on wire rack.

Beat cream cheese and ½ cup of powdered sugar until well blended. Add whipped topping and mix well. Carefully unroll cake, remove towel, and spread cream cheese mixture over cake. Reroll cake, and wrap in plastic wrap. Chill for 1 hour or until ready to serve. Sprinkle with remaining 2 tbsp. powdered sugar just before serving.

Cinnamon Toast Roll-Ups

8 oz. cream cheese, soft

¼ tsp. vanilla

1 tsp. cinnamon

12 slices bread, crusts removed

½ cup sugar, divided

1 egg yolk

3 tbsp. butter, melted

Mix cream cheese, ¼ cup sugar, vanilla, and egg yolk well. Separately mix ¼ cup sugar and cinnamon and set aside. Flatten bread with rolling pin. Spread cream cheese mixture (1 tbsp.) on each slice; roll up tightly. Brush with butter and roll in sugar cinnamon mixture. Slice each roll in 3 pieces. Place seam side down on baking sheet and bake for 12 to 15 minutes at 400°F until golden brown.

Creamy Pumpkin Bars

1 ½ cup graham cracker crumbs

1/3 cup chopped walnuts

¼ cup sugar

½ cup butter, melted

8 oz. cream cheese, soft

2 cups cold milk, divided

16 oz. pumpkin

2 tsp. pumpkin pie spice

8 oz. Cool Whip, divided

2 pkgs. (4 serving-size each) Jell-O vanilla instant pudding and pie filling

Mix crumbs, walnuts, sugar, and butter in 13"× 9" baking dish. Press firmly to bottom of dish. Refrigerate until ready to use. Beat cream cheese in bowl until creamy. Gradually add ½ cup milk; beat until well blended. Add remaining 1 ½ cups milk, dry pudding mixes, pumpkin, and spice. Beat until well blended. Gently stir in half of the Cool Whip and pour over crumb crust. Chill for 2 hours, and cut into 24 bars. Top each piece with a dollop of Cool Whip and serve.

Apple Cranberry Streusel Custard Pie

1 unbaked pie shell

1 tsp. cinnamon

½ cup hot water

1 ½ cups apples, peeled and sliced

½ cup flour

½ cup nuts, chopped

14 oz. sweetened condensed milk

2 eggs, beaten

1 ½ cups fresh cranberries

½ cup brown sugar, packed

¼ cup butter, soft

Preheat oven to 425°F. Combine milk and cinnamon. Beat eggs and add to mixture, then add water and fruits; mix well. Pour into pie shell.

In a bowl, combine sugar, flour, then cut in butter until crumbly. Add nuts to mixture and sprinkle over pie. Bake for 10 minutes. Reduce oven temperature to 375°F and continue baking for 30 to 40 minutes or until golden brown. Cool and serve.

Banana Coconut Cream Pie

Graham Cracker Crumb Crust

2 cups graham cracker crumbs

¼ cup butter, soft

¼ cup sugar

Mix together and press all into pie plate.

Pie Filling

3 tbsp. cornstarch

14 oz. sweetened condensed milk

2 tbsp. butter

½ cup flaked coconut, toasted

lemon juice

1 1/3 cups water

3 egg yolks, beaten

1 tsp. vanilla

2 bananas

Cool Whip

In heavy saucepan, dissolve cornstarch in water; stir in milk and beaten egg yolks. Cook and stir until thick and bubbly. Remove from heat; add butter and vanilla. Cool slightly; fold in coconut. Slice bananas, dip in lemon juice, and drain. Arrange on bottom of pie crust. Pour filling over bananas; cover. Chill for 4 hours or until set. Top with Cool Whip. Garnish with coconut and sliced bananas.

Banana Cream Pie

1 unbaked pie crust
¼ tsp. salt
1 2/3 cups water
3 egg yolks
3 bananas
Cool Whip

3 tbsp. cornstarch
2 tbsp. butter
14 oz. sweetened condensed milk
1 tsp. vanilla
lemon juice

Roll out pie crust and place in pie plate; set aside. In a heavy saucepan, dissolve cornstarch and salt in water; stir in milk and beaten egg yolks. Cook and stir until thick and bubbly. Remove from heat. Add butter, vanilla, and cool slightly. Slice bananas, dip in lemon juice, and drain. Set aside 1 sliced banana for top then place the rest on top of pie crust and pour filling over bananas; cover completely. Chill for 4 hours or until set. Spread top with Cool Whip and banana slices.

Banana Mandarin Cream Cheese Pie

1 Graham Cracker Crust

2 cups graham cracker crumbs
¼ cup butter, soft
¼ cup sugar

Mix together and press into pie plate.

Filling

8 oz. cream cheese, soft

14 oz. sweetened condensed milk

1/3 cup lemon juice + little extra for bananas

1 tsp. vanilla

3 bananas

11 oz. mandarin orange segments, well drained

In a bowl, beat cream cheese until fluffy. Gradually beat in milk until smooth. Stir in 1/3 cup lemon juice and vanilla. Slice bananas, dip in extra lemon juice, and set 1 sliced and dipped banana aside for top. Line crust with bananas and about two-thirds of the oranges. Pour filling over fruit. Chill for 3 hours or until set. Top with remaining bananas and oranges. Chill and serve.

Banana Pudding Cream Pie

1 ½ cups vanilla wafer crumbs

¼ cup sugar

1/3 cup butter, soft

14 oz. sweetened condensed milk

4 egg yolks

½ cup water

1 small pkg. vanilla flavor pudding mix (not instant)

8 oz. sour cream, at room temperature Cool Whip

3 bananas, sliced, dipped in lemon juice and drained

Preheat oven to 375°F. Combine crumbs, sugar, and butter then press into pie plate. Bake for 8 to 10 minutes. Cool. In a heavy saucepan, combine milk, egg yolks, water, pudding mix, and blend well. Over medium heat, cook and stir until thick and bubbly. Cool for 15 minutes. Beat in sour cream. Arrange 2 sliced bananas on top of crust, and pour filling over to cover. Chill for 3 hours. Top with Cool Whip and last of the banana slices.

Black Forest Pie

1 baked pie shell
1 oz. (4 squares) unsweetened chocolate
14 oz. sweetened condensed milk
1 tsp. almond extract
1 ½ cups Cool Whip
21 oz. cherry pie filling, chilled
toasted almonds

In a heavy saucepan, using medium-low heat, melt chocolate with milk. Remove from heat; stir in extract. Pour into bowl; chill. Beat until smooth; fold in Cool Whip. Pour into baked pie shell. Chill for 4 hours or until set. Top with cherries and almonds.

Blueberry Cheesecake Pie

1 unbaked pie shell
2 eggs
8 oz. cream cheese, soft
14 oz. sweetened condensed milk
21 oz. blueberry pie filling
1 tsp. grated lemon rind
1 tsp. vanilla
2 tbsp. lemon juice

Preheat oven to 425°F. Combine 1 cup pie filling with ½ tsp. lemon rind and pour into crust. Bake for 15 minutes; remove from oven. Chill remaining pie filling. In a bowl, beat cream cheese until fluffy; gradually beat in milk, eggs, lemon juice, vanilla, and pour over blueberries. Reduce oven to 350°F and bake for 25 minutes or until set. Chill, serve with remaining chilled pie filling, and top with Cool Whip.

Cherry Lemon Cheesecake Pie

Graham Cracker Crust

2 cups graham cracker crumbs
¼ cup butter
¼ cup sugar

Mix well and press into pie plate.

Filling

8 oz. cream cheese, soft
14 oz. sweetened condensed milk
1/3 cup lemon juice
1 tsp. vanilla
21 oz. cherry pie filling, chilled

Beat cream cheese until fluffy. Gradually beat in milk until smooth. Stir in lemon juice and vanilla. Pour into crust. Chill for 3 hours. Top with cherry pie filling and chill and serve.

Cherry Vanilla Cheesecake Pie Filling

8 oz. cream cheese, soft
¾ cup cold water
1 cup Cool Whip

14 oz. sweetened condensed milk
small pkg. instant vanilla pudding mix
21 oz. cherry pie filling

In a bowl, beat cream cheese until light and fluffy. Gradually beat in milk until smooth. Beat in cold water and pudding mix until smooth. Chill for 30 minutes. Fold in Cool Whip.

Pour over crust half of the cream cheese mixture, next half cherry pie filling, then last half of cream cheese mixture, and top with last of cherry pie filling. Chill for 3 hours or until set.

This is great with either graham cracker crust or traditional pie crust.

Chocolate Peanut Butter Mousse Pie

1 cup chocolate graham cracker crumbs
6 tbsp. butter, soft
1/3 cup honey-roasted peanuts, finely chopped
1 + ½ cups whipping cream, divided
1 ½ cup chocolate chips
14 oz, sweetened condensed milk, divided
6 oz. cream cheese, soft
¾ cup creamy peanut butter

In a medium bowl, combine cracker crumbs, butter, and peanuts. Press into pie plate; set aside. Heat ½ cup whipping cream over medium-low heat until hot. Stir ½ cup milk and all chocolate chips stirring until smooth; remove from heat. Spoon mixture into crust. Chill for 1 hour.

In a large bowl, beat remaining whipping cream until stiff peaks form; set aside. In a small bowl, beat remaining milk, cream cheese, and peanut butter until smooth; fold in whipped cream. Spoon over chocolate filling. Freeze for 4 hours or until firm.

Let stand for 15 minutes before serving. Store leftovers covered in freezer.

Cocoa Peanut Butter Chip Pie

1 crust of choice
¼ cup butter
14 oz. sweetened condensed milk
1 egg, beaten
1 + 1/4 cup peanut butter chips
¼ cup unsweetened cocoa
1/3 cup water
½ tsp. vanilla whipped cream

Preheat oven to 350°F. Sprinkle 1 cup of chips on bottom of crust. In a saucepan, over low heat, melt butter, add cocoa, and stir until smooth. Add milk and water and mix well. Cook for about 5 minutes; stir until smooth. Remove from heat; stir in egg and vanilla. Pour into crust; may use graham cracker or chocolate cookie crust. Bake for 30 minutes or until edges are set; center will firm up while cooling. Cool pie, spread with whipped cream, and garnish with chips.

Coconut Custard Pie

1 baked pie crust of choice

3 eggs

14 oz. sweetened condensed milk

1/8 tsp. nutmeg

1 cup flaked coconut

¼ tsp. salt

1 ¼ cup hot water

Preheat oven to 425°F. Toast ½ cup coconut; set aside. In bowl, beat eggs; then add milk, water, vanilla, salt, nutmeg; and mix well. Stir in remaining ½ cup coconut. Pour into baked pie shell. Sprinkle with toasted coconut. Bake for 10 minutes. Reduce oven to 350°F, and bake for 25 to 30 minutes longer or until inserted knife comes out clean. Cool before cutting.

Cranberry Crumb Pie

1 unbaked pie crust

¼ cup lemon juice

1 + 2 tbsp. brown sugar

16 oz. whole berry cranberry sauce

1/3 cup flour

8 oz. cream cheese

14 oz. sweetened condensed milk

2 tbsp. cornstarch

¼ cup butter

¾ cup chopped walnuts

Preheat oven to 425°F. Bake pie crust for 6 minutes and remove from oven. Reduce oven temperature to 375°F. In a bowl, beat cream cheese and lemon juice until fluffy. Slowly beat in milk until smooth; pour into pie crust.

Combine 1 tbsp. brown sugar, cornstarch, and mix well. Stir in cranberry sauce; spoon over cheese mixture. Crumble together butter, 2 tbsp. brown sugar; stir in walnuts. Top cranberry mixture; bake for 45 to 50 minutes until bubbly and golden. Cool; serve.

Creamy Chocolate Pie

3 oz. chocolate chips

¼ tsp. salt

2 egg yolks

1 cup Cool Whip

1 baked pie crust

14 oz. sweetened condensed milk

¼ cup hot water

1 tsp. vanilla

Cool Whip for garnish

In heavy saucepan, over medium heat, melt chocolate with milk and salt until thick and bubbly, 5 to 8 minutes. Add water and egg yolks, cook stirring constantly until mixture is thick and bubbly again. Remove from heat, stir in vanilla. Chill 30 minutes, then stir. In bowl fold together Cool Whip and chilled chocolate mixture. Pour into pie crust. Chill 3 hours or until set. Garnish with additional whip cream, chill.

Creamy Lemon Pie

1 baked pie crust

14 oz. sweetened condensed milk

Cool Whip

3 egg yolks

½ cup lemon juice

Lemon zest

Preheat oven to 325°F. Beat egg yolks in bowl with fork; gradually beat in milk and lemon juice. Pour into crust. Bake for 30 to 35 minutes or until set. Remove from oven. Cool for 3 hours. Spread Cool Whip over pie, and garnish with lemon zest.

Decadent Brownie Pie

1 unbaked pie shell

¼ cup butter

½ cup biscuit baking mix (p. 93)

1 tsp. vanilla

vanilla ice cream

1 cup chocolate chips

14 oz. sweetened condensed milk

2 eggs

1 cup nuts, chopped

Preheat oven to 375°F. Bake pie shell for 10 minutes and remove from oven. Reduce oven temperature to 325°F. In a saucepan over low heat, melt chips and butter. In bowl, beat chocolate mixture with milk, biscuit mix, eggs, and vanilla until smooth. Add nuts. Pour into pie shell. Bake for 35 to 40 minutes or until set. Serve warm with ice cream.

Easter Candy Pie

8 oz. cream cheese   14 oz. sweetened condensed milk
¾ cup cold water   small pkg. instant pudding mix
1 ½ cups Cool Whip   1 graham cracker crust
16 small chocolate eggs or jelly beans candy for garnish also

In a bowl, beat cream cheese until fluffy. Gradually beat in milk until smooth. Add water and pudding mix; beat until smooth. Gently fold in Cool Whip. Spoon half of filling into pie crust. Top with candy and last half of filling. Garnish with candy.

Frozen Cherry or Berry Cream Pie

2 graham cracker or chocolate pie crusts
8 oz. cream cheese, soft
14 oz. sweetened condensed milk
1 tbsp. lemon juice
2 cups frozen sweet cherries, chopped or berries
splash of almond extract
8 oz. Cool Whip

In bowl, beat cream cheese until fluffy. Gradually beat in milk until smooth. Mix in cherries or berries, lemon juice, and almond extract. Fold in Cool Whip. Pour mixture into crusts and freeze overnight. Let stand for 5 minutes before serving. Freeze leftovers.

Frozen Chocolate Mousse Pie

2 cups finely crushed crème-filled chocolate cookies, about 20
¼ cup butter, soft
1 cup chocolate chips
1 ½ tsp. vanilla
14 oz. sweetened condensed milk
1 cup Cool Whip

Combine crumbs and butter and press into pie plate and chill. Over low heat, melt chocolate chips, stirring until smooth. Remove from heat; mix in milk and vanilla until smooth. Chill for 15 minutes then fold in Cool Whip and pour into crust. Freeze overnight (minimum of 6 hours). Freeze leftovers

Frozen Peanut Butter Pie

8 oz. cream cheese, soft
14 oz. sweetened condensed milk
¾ cup peanut butter
2 tbsp. lemon juice
1 tsp. vanilla
1 cup Cool Whip
1 Chocolate Crunch Crust (see below)
fudge ice cream topping

In a bowl, beat cream cheese until fluffy; gradually beat in milk and then peanut butter until smooth. Stir in lemon juice and vanilla. Fold in Cool Whip and turn into chilled chocolate crunch crust. Drizzle fudge ice cream topping over pie. Freeze overnight or 4 hours minimum.

Chocolate Crunch Crust. In a heavy saucepan over low heat, melt 1/3 cup butter and 6 oz. chocolate chips. Remove from heat; gently stir in 2 ½ cups of oven-toasted rice cereal until completely coated. Press on bottom and up side to rim of buttered pie plate. Chill for 30 minutes.

Glazed Apple Custard Pie

1 pie crust, unbaked
1 ½ cups sour cream
¼ tsp. cinnamon
14 oz. sweetened condensed milk
1 egg
1 ½ tsp. vanilla
¼ cup frozen apple juice concentrate, thawed
butter
3 medium apples, cored, pared, and sliced
Apple Cinnamon Glaze (see below)

Preheat oven to 375°F and bake pie crust for 15 minutes. In a bowl, beat sour cream, cinnamon, milk, apple juice, egg, and vanilla until smooth. Pour into baked pie shell. Bake for 30 minutes or until set. Cool. In a skillet, cook apples in butter until tender crisp. Arrange on top of pie, and drizzle with Apple Cinnamon Glaze.

Apple Cinnamon Glaze. In a saucepan, combine ¼ cup thawed frozen apple juice concentrate, 1 tsp. cornstarch, and ¼ tsp. ground cinnamon. Mix well. Over low heat, cook and stir until thick. Makes about ¼ cup.

Key Lime Pie

3 eggs, separated
½ cup lime juice
¼ tsp. cream of tartar

14 oz. sweetened condensed milk
1 unbaked pie crust
1/3 cup sugar

Preheat oven at 325°F. In a bowl, beat egg yolks. Gradually beat in milk and lime juice until smooth. Pour mixture into pie crust and bake for 30 minutes. Remove from oven and increase oven to 350°F.

Meringue. In bowl, beat egg whites and cream of tartar until peaks form. Gradually beat in sugar, 1 teaspoon at a time; beat for 4 minutes longer or until sugar is dissolved and stiff and glossy peaks form. Spread immediately over hot pie; carefully seal to edge of crust to prevent meringue from shrinking. Bake for 15 minutes; let cool for 1 hour. Chill for at least 3 hours.

Lemon Ice Box Pie

1 crust of choice   14 oz. sweetened condensed milk
½ cup lemon juice   1 cup whipped cream

In a bowl, stir together milk and juice until creamy. Fold in whipped cream. Pour into crust and chill for 3 hours or until set.

Maple Walnut Pumpkin Pie

1 unbaked pie shell   14 oz. sweetened condensed milk
2 cups pumpkin   2 eggs
1 tsp. maple flavor   1 tsp. cinnamon
½ tsp. salt   ¼ tsp. ginger
¼ tsp. nutmeg   1/3 cup brown sugar, firmly packed
1/3 cup flour   3 tbsp. butter
½ cup walnuts

Preheat oven to 425°F. In a bowl combine pumpkin, milk, eggs, maple, ½ tsp. cinnamon, ginger, nutmeg, and salt, mix well, pour into pie shell, and bake for 15 minutes. Reduce oven to 350°F and continue baking for 30 minutes. In a bowl, combine sugar, flour, and remaining ½ tsp. cinnamon. Cut in butter until crumbly. Stir in nuts, remove pie from oven and top with crumb mixture, and continue baking for 10 minutes. Cool and serve.

Minty Grasshopper Pie

8 oz. cream cheese, soft

green food coloring

8 oz. Cool Whip

14 oz. sweetened condensed milk

16 fudge mint cookies, coarsely crushed

1 chocolate pie crust

Beat cream cheese until fluffy; gradually beat in milk until smooth. Stir in food coloring then crushed cookies. Fold in whipped topping. Pour into crust. Chill for 3 hours or until set. Serve chilled.

Mocha Walnut Pie

1 unbaked pie shell

¼ cup butter

14 oz. sweetened condensed milk

1 tsp. vanilla

whipped topping

2 oz. chocolate chips

¼ cup hot coffee (strong)

2 eggs, well beaten

1 cup walnuts, chopped

Preheat oven to 350°F. In a saucepan over low heat, melt chocolate and butter. Stir in coffee, milk, eggs, vanilla, and mix well. Pour into pie shell, top with walnuts, and bake for 40 to 45 minutes or until set. Top with whipped cream.

Perfect Pumpkin Pie

2 cups pumpkin

2 eggs

½ tsp. ginger

½ tsp. salt

14 oz. sweetened condensed milk

1 tsp. cinnamon

½ tsp. nutmeg

1 unbaked pie crust

Preheat oven to 425°F. Mix pumpkin, milk, eggs, spices, and salt until smooth. Pour into crust. Bake for 15 minutes. Reduce oven to 350°F and continue baking for 35 minutes or until knife comes out clean. Cool and serve.

Peppermint Pie

¼ cup chocolate cookie crumbs

14 oz. sweetened condensed milk

1 cup crushed hard peppermint candy

8 oz. cream cheese, soft

red food coloring, optional

8 oz. whipped cream

Butter pie plate and sprinkle cookie crumbs on sides and bottom of plate. In a bowl, beat cream cheese until fluffy. Gradually beat in milk until smooth. Stir in candy and food coloring (if using). Fold in whipped cream and pour into pie plate. Cover and freeze for 6 hours (minimum) until firm. (I usually do overnight.)

Sweet Potato Pie

1 unbaked pie crust

¼ cup butter

1 tsp. vanilla

1 tsp. cinnamon

¼ tsp. salt

whipped cream topping

1 lb. sweet potatoes, cooked and peeled

14 oz. sweetened condensed milk

1 tsp. grated orange rind

1 tsp. nutmeg

2 eggs

Preheat oven to 350°F. In a bowl, beat sweet potatoes and butter until smooth. Add milk, vanilla, orange rind, cinnamon, nutmeg, salt, and eggs; mix well. Pour into pie shell and bake for 30 minutes or until golden brown; cool. And top with whipped cream.

Sweet Potato Pecan Pie

Follow directions to Sweet Potato Pie and top with Pecan Topping. Beat 1 egg, 2 tbsp. dark corn syrup and 2 tbsp. packed brown sugar, 1 tbsp. melted butter, and ½ tsp. maple flavoring. Stir in 1 cup chopped pecans. Bake; cool.

Dutch Apple Dessert

5 medium apples, pared, cored, and sliced thinly
14 oz. sweetened condensed milk
1 tsp. cinnamon
½ cup + 2 tbsp. butter
1 + ½ cup biscuit baking mix (see p. 93)
½ cup brown sugar, packed
½ cup chopped nuts
vanilla ice cream

Preheat oven to 325°F. In a bowl, combine apples, milk, and cinnamon. In another bowl, cut ½ cup butter into 1 cup biscuit mix until crumbly. Stir in apple mixture. Pour into greased square baking dish. In another bowl, combine remaining ½ cup biscuit mix and brown sugar; cut in 2 tbsp. butter until crumbly. Add nuts and sprinkle over apple mixture and bake for 1 hour or until golden brown. Serve warm with vanilla ice cream.

Caramel Sauce

1 cup sugar
¼ cup water
1 cup heavy cream

In a saucepan, combine sugar and water and bring to a boil, stirring often until mixture is a deep caramel color and has the consistency of thin syrup for about 10 to 15 minutes. Remove from heat. Stir in cream, return to heat on high, and boil the sauce until it is the consistency of thick syrup for about 2 minutes. Cool.

Pecan Topping

Beat together 1 egg, 2 tbsp. dark corn syrup and 2 tbsp. firmly packed brown sugar, 1 tbsp. melted butter, and ½ tsp. maple flavoring. Stir in 1 cup chopped pecans.

Sour Cream Topping

In a bowl, combine 1 ½ cups sour cream, 2 tbsp. sugar, and 1 tsp. vanilla extract. After pie has baked for 30 minutes at 350°F, spread evenly over top and bake for 10 minutes.

Chocolate Glaze

In a saucepan over low heat, melt ½ cup chocolate chips and 1 tsp. shortening or butter. Drizzle or spread over top of baked pie or pastry.

Walnut Crumble Topping

In a bowl, combine 1/3 cup packed brown sugar, 1/3 cup flour, ½ tsp. cinnamon. Cut in 3 tbsp. cold butter until crumbly. Stir in ½ cup chopped walnuts. Great for pies or muffins.

Apple Cinnamon Glaze

In a saucepan, combine ¼ cup thawed frozen apple juice concentrate, 1 tsp. cornstarch, and ¼ tsp. cinnamon. Mix well. Over low heat, cook stirring until thick. Makes ¼ cup.

Meringue

In a large bowl, beat with mixer on high 3 egg whites and ¼ tsp. cream of tartar until peaks form. Gradually beat in, on medium speed, 1/3 cup sugar, 1 tsp. at a time. Beat for 4 minutes or until sugar is dissolved and stiff, glossy peaks form. Spread meringue over hot pie, carefully sealing to edge of crust to prevent meringue from shrinking. Bake for 15 minutes at 325°F. Let cool for 1 hour. Chill for at least 3 hours before serving.

Hot Fudge Topping

¼ lb. butter

2 cups powdered sugar

1 tsp. vanilla

¾ cup chocolate chips

1 can evaporated milk

Melt together the butter and chocolate chips slowly in a saucepan. Add the powdered sugar and milk. Stir all together and bring to a boil. Boil for 8 minutes. Remove from heat and add vanilla. Stir and put into pint jars. Store in refrigerator. Heat and serve over ice cream.

Homemade Twinkies

1 yellow cake mix

1 cup milk

½ cup butter

1 tsp. vanilla

5 tbsp. flour

½ cup shortening

½ tsp. salt

1 cup sugar

Bake cake mix according to directions in a 17"× 20" baking sheet lined with wax paper. Cool and cut cake in half. Wax paper will peel off easily. Cook in a saucepan the flour and milk until thick, stirring constantly, Cool. Beat shortening, butter, salt, vanilla and sugar until fluffy. Stir flour mixture well, slowly add to sugar mix. Beat until very fluffy. Put filling between layers of cake and dust with powdered sugar. Refrigerate. Also good with chocolate cake for Suzy Q's.

Homemade Mints

butter

2 cups sugar

3 tbsp. butter

ice

1 cup water

food color cherry, mint, or spearmint oil flavoring

Candy thermometer, marble slab, cold kitchen scissors

Before cooking, butter the marble slab and cover with ice. Also make sure scissors are in the refrigerator getting cold.

Combine sugar, water, and butter in a large pot. Stir and cook on high until temperature reaches 240°F. Continue cooking and stirring, but remove ice from slab and wipe it down. Stir constantly from 240 to 258°F because it will cook quickly. Remove from heat at 258°F and pour the mixture onto the slab. Add 3 to 4 drops of color and 8 to 10 drops of flavoring. After a minute or so, spread corners out to side and fold it over while moving it across slab. After cool enough to handle, twist and pull for 10 minutes. Cut with cold kitchen scissors into small pieces onto wax paper on baking sheet. Refrigerate for 30 minutes. Remove and let it become cream overnight.

Makes 1 pound of candy. Cool your hands before pulling.

Basic Homemade Mix for Cake

4 + 4 cups sifted all-purpose flour   2 cups shortening
5 cups sugar   4 tsp. salt
¼ cup baking powder

In a very large bowl, turn 4 cups flour. Add shortening, 4 cups flour, sugar, baking powder, and salt. With a pastry blender, cut in shortening until crumbly. Store in airtight container in refrigerator up to 6 months. Makes 15 cups. (If using self-rising flour, omit baking powder and salt.)

Upside-Down Cocktail Cake

¼ cup butter   ½ cup brown sugar
1 can fruit cocktail, well drained   ½ cup finely chopped walnuts
2 ½ cup homemade cake mix   ½ + ¼ cup milk
1 egg   ½ tsp. vanilla

Melt butter over low heat in round 9-inch pan; remove from heat. Sprinkle with brown sugar; spoon fruit cocktail and nuts evenly over sugar and reserve. Turn cake mix into a small mixing bowl. Add ½ cup milk and stir to blend. Beat 2 minutes at medium speed. Add remaining ¼ cup milk, egg, and vanilla and blend well. Beat for 2 minutes; turn batter into prepared pan. Bake at 350°F for 45 to 50 minutes or until toothpick comes out clean. Cool for 5 minutes before turning out of pan.

Raisin Spice Cake

4 cup homemade cake mix

½ tsp. cloves

2 eggs

½ cup raisins

1 tsp. cinnamon

½ + ¼ cup milk

1 tbsp. light molasses

Stir cinnamon and cloves into cake mix. Add ½ cup milk; blend well. Beat for 2 minutes on medium speed. Add ¼ cup milk, eggs, and molasses. Blend well. Beat for 2 minutes. Stir in raisins. Bake in 9-inch greased pan at 350°F for 35 to 40 minutes or until done. Turn out and cool.

Layer Cake

4 cup homemade cake mix

1 cup milk

2 eggs

1 tsp. vanilla

Blend all well. Grease 2 layer greased pans. Bake at 350°F for 25 to 30 minutes.

Homemade Candy

1 lb. powdered sugar	1 cup butter
7 oz. flake coconut	2 tsp. salt
14 oz. sweetened condensed milk	2 cups pecans
12 oz. maraschino cherries	12 oz. chocolate chips
paraffin	

Mix sugar, butter, coconut, salt, milk, chopped pecans, and chopped cherries and chill overnight. Pinch into small balls (size of a walnut). Dust hands with powdered sugar to mold balls in shape. Chill for 1 hour.

Icing

Melt 12 oz. chocolate chips and 1 block paraffin over low heat. Drop in balls one at a time while icing is hot. Remove and place on wax paper. Makes 70 balls.

Homemade Chocolate-Covered Cherries

1/3 cup light corn syrup	1 lb. powdered sugar
1/3 cup butter	16 oz. maraschino cherries, drained
12 oz. chocolate chips	½ bar paraffin

At room temperature, mix syrup, powdered sugar, and butter by hand until it forms a nice ball. Form dough as thin as possible around each cherry. Place on wax paper on cookie sheet and chill in freezer for 30 minutes to harden. Over low heat, melt chocolate chips and paraffin. Stick a toothpick in a cherry ball and dip quickly into chocolate and drop into small candy wrapper. After all are formed, drizzle chocolate over top to cover toothpick hole. Let set a few days in refrigerator before eating. Makes about 100.

Homemade Cracker Jacks

1 cup brown sugar

¼ cup light Karo syrup

½ tsp. soda

1 cup skinless raw peanuts

½ cup butter

½ tsp. salt

3 to 4 quarts popped corn

Combine first 4 ingredients. Melt in microwave full power for 2 minutes; stir in soda. Spray paper bag well with cooking spray. Pour mixture over popped corn in paper bag; cook in microwave 30 seconds. Shake and cook 90 seconds more. Spread onto cookie sheet.

Homemade Banana Pudding

2 cups sugar

3 egg yolks, well beaten

¼ cup butter

bananas wafers

3 tbsp. self-rising flour

3 ½ cups milk

1 tsp. vanilla

Pudding

Mix sugar and flour in a saucepan; add milk and eggs yolks. Cook over low heat, stirring constantly until it thickens. Add butter and vanilla. Let cool. Layer bananas and wafers in a baking dish. Pour pudding over them, and let it soak in.

Topping

3 egg whites

¾ cup sugar

1 tsp. vanilla

Beat egg whites until stiff. Add sugar and vanilla and beat well. Pour over pudding. Place under broiler until light brown. Chill until ready to serve.

Homemade Popsicles

3 oz. regular Jell-O   2 cups boiling water
1 small pkg. Kool-Aid, unsweetened   1 cup sugar
2 cups cold water

Bring 2 cups water to boil, add Jell-O, Kool-Aid, and sugar. Stir until dissolved. Add 2 cups cold water. Place in molds and freeze.

Homemade Cake from Scratch

1 cup butter   2 cups sugar   4 eggs
1 cup milk   3 cups flour   1 tbsp. baking powder
1 tsp. vanilla extract 1 tsp. lemon extract

Cream butter and sugar until creamy. Add eggs one at a time. Add milk, flavorings, flour, and baking powder. Stir until blended. Whip until light and creamy. Bake at 350°F until cake comes from side of pan.

Homemade Brownie Mix

4 cups flour   4 ½ cups sugar
1 cup cocoa   1 ½ cups dry milk
1 ½ tbsp. baking powder   1 ½ tsp. salt

Mix well and keep in refrigerator in a canister.

To make brownies. Mix together 1 ¾ cups brownie mix, 1 egg, ¼ cup warm water, ½ cup oil, 1 tsp. vanilla, ¼ cup melted butter, and 2 eggs. Bake 20 minutes at 350°F in 9"× 9" baking dish. Serve hot with ice cream.

Homemade Chocolate Crisp Candy

24 oz. semisweet chocolate chips   12 oz. milk chocolate chips
1 tbsp. butter   1 ½ cups Rice Krispies cereal

Melt semisweet chips and butter in a saucepan over low heat until smooth. Remove from heat. Add milk chips and cereal. Spread on a cookie sheet lined with wax paper.

Put in freezer for 10 minutes or until set. Remove and cut into desired shapes with cookie cutter and serve.

Homemade Frozen Custard Cones

2/3 cup sugar   1 ½ tbsp. flour
1 tbsp. cornstarch   dash of salt
2 cups milk   2 egg yolks, slightly beaten
1 ½ tsp. vanilla   2 cups whipped cream

Mix flour, cornstarch, sugar, and salt in a saucepan and add milk slowly, stirring until smooth. Cook over medium-low heat until slightly thick. Take out a little of the hot mix and stir in egg yolks. Stir egg mix with hot custard. Cook for 2 minutes but *not* to a boil. Remove from heat; add vanilla. Put into freezing tray and freeze until mushy. Beat a few minutes and fold in whipped cream until firm. Let soften a few minute and scoop into cups or cones.

Homemade Hard Candy

3 ¾ cups sugar   1 ¼ cups Karo syrup
1 cup water   food coloring
1 tsp. oil flavoring, cinnamon or peppermint   powdered sugar

Sprinkle powdered sugar on large cookie sheet. Mix sugar, syrup, and water in a saucepan. Stir over medium heat until sugar dissolves. Boil, without stirring, until temperature reaches 310°F and mixture forms hard brittle threads in cold water. Remove from heat; stir in flavoring and color. Pour on cookie sheet and sprinkle with powdered sugar. Cool and break into pieces. Store in airtight ziplock bags.

Homemade Heath Bars

saltine crackers

1 cup sugar

12 oz. milk chocolate chips

1 cup butter

pecans, chopped

Line a cookie sheet with foil. Cover bottom with crackers. Melt butter in a saucepan. Add sugar and bring to boil for 3 minutes. Pour over crackers and spread with knife or spatula to cover. Bake at 350°F for 15 minutes. Remove from heat and sprinkle with chocolate chips over crackers. Bake until melted; smooth over top of crackers covering completely. Add chopped pecans to top and chill to cool completely. Break into pieces.

Homemade Peppermints

1 egg white

1 tbsp. canned milk

2 ¼ cups powdered sugar

1 tsp. peppermint flavoring or 4 drops of peppermint oil

Mix egg white and milk. Slowly add powdered sugar and beat well. Add peppermint flavoring or oil. Drop onto wax paper by ¼ tsp. or mold into desired shape.

Homemade Marshmallows

1 large pkg. Jell-O	1 ½ cup boiling water
½ cup corn syrup	sugar

In mixing bowl, mix Jell-O and boiling water; stir until all is dissolved. Add corn syrup and mix well. Cool mixture in refrigerator until thick. Whip with mixer until fluffy. Pour into baking pan and let set until firm. Cut into cubes and roll in sugar. For variations, use different flavors of Jell-O.

Homemade Coconut Marshmallows

2 envelopes plain gelatin	2/3 cups water
1 cup sugar	1 1/3 cup white Karo syrup
2 tsp. vanilla	14 oz. toasted coconut

In a saucepan, dissolve gelatin in water over low heat. Add sugar; stir until dissolved. In a large bowl, mix Karo syrup and vanilla. Add gelatin mixture and beat for 15 minutes. In 9"× 13" baking dish, sprinkle toasted coconut. Pour mixture over coconut and top with coconut. Let stand for 1 hour, not in refrigerator.

To remove from pan, loosen from edges with knife and place over large cutting board. Cut into squares and cover sides with coconut.

Homemade Marshmallow Crème

2 + 1/2 cups Karo syrup	2 cups sugar
1 cup water	1 cup egg whites
4 tsp. vanilla	

Cook 2 cups Karo syrup, sugar, and water to 240°F; set aside. In a large bowl, beat egg whites and ½ cup Karo syrup until mixed well. Beat by hand until light and fluffy. Slowly add hot syrup while beating. When all is mixed, beat hard for 3 minutes. Add vanilla.

Homemade Chocolate Covered Mints

1 cube butter
14 oz. sweetened condensed milk
semisweet chocolate for dipping

4 tsp. mint extract
3 lbs. powdered sugar

Cream butter, extract, and milk until smooth. Slowly add sugar, mixing with hands. Roll into balls. Between palms, flatten on cookie sheet. Freeze. Drop in melted chocolate to cover. Freeze and store in a jar until needed.

Homemade Munchies

Line cookie tray with foil. Top with club crackers to cover tray. Sprinkle top with slivered almonds. In a saucepan, melt 2/3 cup sugar and ½ lb. butter and sprinkle over crackers. Bake for 15 to 20 minutes at 300°F.

Homemade Mounds Bars

1 ½ cup light corn syrup
14 oz. coconut, shredded
12 oz. chocolate chips
¾ bar paraffin

Boil syrup for 1 minute and add coconut. Mix well. Remove from heat. Let stand for 2 hours. Wet hands and form into balls. Freeze. In a saucepan, melt chocolate chips and paraffin together and dip in coconut balls. Place on wax paper.

Homemade Oreo Cookies

1 devil's food cake mix
½ cup butter
2 eggs

Mix all together and roll the dough into dime-sized balls and place on cookie sheet. Bake at 350°F for 8 minutes. Cool cookies.

Frosting

8 oz. cream cheese
½ pat butter
2 tsp. vanilla
4 cups powdered sugar

Mix all until smooth. Frost backs of cookies and sandwich them.

Homemade Orange Sherbet

3 oz. pkg. orange Jell-O   2 cups boiling water
1 cup sugar   1 ½ cups milk

Dissolve in water the Jell-O and sugar; add milk. Beat up and put in plastic bowl and freeze until quite firm. Beat real well and put in container. Store in freezer.

Homemade Pay Day

1 cup light corn syrup   1 cup sugar
1 cup salted peanuts   1 cup peanut butter
12 oz. semisweet chocolate chips 6 cups Rice Chex cereal

Bring corn syrup and sugar to boil. Remove from heat and add peanuts and peanut butter. Stir until smooth. Add chips and stir until melted. Add cereal and mix well. Spread in 9"× 13" pan. Cool and break into bite-sized pieces. Store in tightly covered container.

Homemade Peanut Butter Cups

12 oz. chocolate chips

3 dozen 1-inch paper cups

¾ cup sifted powdered sugar

2 tbsp. shortening

¾ cup creamy peanut butter

1 tbsp. melted butter

Chocolate cups. Using a double boiler, melt chips and shortening until smooth. Remove from heat but leave over hot water. Coat the inside of each cup with 1 tsp. chocolate. Place cups in palm of hand, rotating gently while pushing chocolate up sides with a spoon or rubber spatula. Chill until firm.

Peanut butter filling. In a small bowl, mix peanut butter, powdered sugar, and melted butter. Form into small balls and place into chilled cups. Press ball down to fill and spoon chocolate to seal edges. Chill for one hour. Store in refrigerator.

Homemade Salted Nut Rolls

7 oz. marshmallow crème

3 tbsp. water

1 small can salted peanuts, chopped

2 ¼ cups powdered sugar

17 oz. caramels

Knead together marshmallow crème and powdered sugar. Shape into small fingers, put on cookie sheet, and freeze. In a double boiler, melt together caramels and water. Dip crème fingers into caramel mixture and roll in chopped peanuts. Freeze until set and refrigerate until eaten.

Homemade Russell Stover Candies

2 cups powdered sugar

¼ cup coconut

12 oz. chocolate chips

14 oz. sweetened condensed milk

½ lb. shortening, not butter

Mix sugar, milk, coconut, and shortening and chill overnight. In a saucepan, melt chocolate chips over low heat. Form filling mixture into small balls. Dip in melted chocolate and set on wax paper to harden. Do NOT REFRIGERATE.

Homemade Reese's Squares

1 cup butter

6 oz. chocolate morsels

1 lb. powdered sugar

2 cups creamy peanut butter

1 ¼ cup graham cracker crumbs

In a saucepan, melt butters. Add cracker crumbs and sugar; mix well. Press into 9"× 13" baking dish. Melt chocolate morsels and spread over mixture in pan. Cool and cut.

Homemade Pudding Pops

1 small pkg. instant pudding mix

1 cup Cool Whip

2 cups cold milk

popsicle molds

Combine pudding mix and milk. Beat until smooth. Add 1 cup Cool Whip and blend well. Pour into molds and freeze

Homemade Snicker Bars

14 oz. lite caramels

2/3 cup sweetened condensed milk, divided

1 German chocolate cake mix

¾ cup melted butter

1 cup nuts, chopped

1 cup semisweet chocolate bits (6 oz.)

In a saucepan, melt caramels and 1/3 cup condensed milk and set aside. In a bowl, combine cake mix, butter, nuts, and remaining condensed milk. Stir until mixed well and crumbly. Press ½ the dough into a 9"× 13" baking dish and bake at 350°F for 6 minutes. Remove from oven and sprinkle chocolate bits evenly over baked dough; quickly spread melted caramel mixture on top. Crumble remaining ½ dough over caramels and press lightly. Return to oven and bake for 14 to 18 minutes until top is set and pulls away from sides of pan. Cool and refrigerate until firm. Cut into 24 squares.

Homemade Bars Like Snickers

First Layer

1 cup chocolate chips
½ cup butterscotch chips

Melt chips and pour into bottom of 9"× 13" baking dish. Freeze to harden for about 10 minutes.

Second Layer

1 cup sugar
¼ cup milk
¼ cup butter
¼ cup peanut butter
1 cup marshmallow crème
1 tsp. vanilla

Boil milk, sugar, and butter for 5 minutes. Add peanut butter, marshmallow crème, and vanilla. Pour over first layer and sprinkle with salted peanuts.

Third Layer

40 caramels
2 tbsp. water

Melt and pour over peanuts.

Fourth Layer

1 cup milk chocolate chips
½ cup butterscotch chips
½ cup peanut butter

Melt chips and peanut butter until smooth. Pour over the top. Cool and chill.

Homemade Candy Like Snickers

12 oz. milk chocolate morsels	2 tbsp. shortening
14 oz. caramels	5 tbsp. butter
2 tbsp. water	1 cup coarsely chopped peanuts

In a saucepan over low heat, melt chocolate morsels and shortening until smooth. Remove from heat but leave over double boiler. Pour half of melted chocolate into 8"× 8" baking dish lined with foil. Spread evenly. Refrigerate until firm for about 15 minutes. Return remaining chocolate mixture to low heat. In double boiler, combine caramels, butter, and water. Stir until caramels are melted smooth. Stir in nuts and blend well. Pour into the chocolate-lined pan. Spread evenly. Refrigerate until tacky for about 15 minutes. Top with remaining melted chocolate; spread evenly over caramel filling and return to refrigerator and chill until firm for at least 1 hour. Cut into small pieces and chill until ready to serve. Makes about 2 ½ dozen candies.

Homemade Taffy

2 cups honey or syrup	2 cups sugar
2/3 cup water	1 tsp. salt

Boil water, honey, and sugar to hard ball stage (288°F).

Put in buttered pans, and let cool enough to handle, then pull. Cut and wrap.

Homemade Turtles

1 cup pecan halves
36 caramels
2 oz. candy chocolate, melted

Place nuts in cluster on cookie sheet. Put 1 caramel on each cluster. Place in oven at 325°F for 8 minutes.

Remove from oven, flatten caramel, and frost with melted chocolate.

Homemade Suckers

2 cups sugar
2/3 cup water
oil flavoring

2/3 cup white corn syrup
food coloring

Mix together until dissolved. Cook at 300°F. Add red food coloring before it reaches 300°F. Remove from heat, and add ½ tsp. cinnamon oil. Stir. Cool slightly. Pour from tablespoon onto sucker sticks arranged on butter pan. Makes about 16 suckers. For variations, use black color and anise oil or orange color and orange oil, or green color and peppermint oil.

Homemade Tasty Kake Kandy Kakes

1/3 cup oil
4 eggs, beaten
2 tsp. butter, melted
2 cups flour
peanut butter

2 cups sugar
1 cup milk
2 tsp. baking powder
12 oz. chocolate chips

Preheat oven to 350°F. Grease a cookie sheet. Mix together oil, sugar, beaten eggs, milk, melted butter, baking powder, and flour. Pour onto cookie sheet. Bake for 18 to 20 minutes. Remove from heat. Spread with peanut butter and refrigerate. When cool, melt 12 oz. chocolate chips and spread on top. Cut into serving sizes before chocolate cools completely.

Homemade Tea Cakes

3 cups flour	½ tsp. baking soda
½ tsp. baking powder	1 cup butter
2 eggs	1 cup sugar
1 tsp. lemon or vanilla extract	

In a bowl, sift flour, baking soda, and baking powder. Cut in butter until it resembles cornmeal. In another bowl, beat eggs, sugar, and flavoring. Add to flour mixture. Chill dough. Roll to 1/8-inch thick. Cut with cookie cutter and sprinkle with sugar. Bake at 375°F for 6 to 8 minutes. Makes 6 dozen.

Homemade Sticky Buns

2 cups warm water (not hot, 110 to 115°F)	2 pkgs. dry yeast
2 tsp. salt	1 egg
½ cup sugar	¼ cup shortening, melted
about 7 cups flour	4 tbsp. butter
½ cup brown sugar	cinnamon

In a bowl, dissolve yeast in water. Stir in sugar, salt, shortening, and eggs. Measure flour and add one cup at a time. Mix by hand until dough is easy to handle, about 6 cups usually. Put into greased bowl, grease top of dough, cover with cloth, and let rise until double in size. Put on well-floured board and roll out to about 1/3-inch thick. Melt butter and spread over top of dough then sprinkle ½ cup brown sugar and cinnamon on dough. Roll up dough and cut into 1-inch-thick pieces. In an oblong baking pan, pour topping mixture (see below), then sprinkle with chopped pecans or walnuts, then place rolls on top of topping mixture. Let rise to double in size then bake at 350°F for 25 to 30 minutes.

Topping

1 ½ cup brown sugar	2 tbsp. water
2 tsp. cinnamon	1 cup butter
1 cup chopped pecans or walnuts	

Mix sugar, butter, and water in ¼ cup water a saucepan. Heat until butter is melted.

Homemade Susie Q's

2 cups flour	2 egg yolks
½ cup shortening	1 cup sugar
1 tsp. vanilla	1 cup milk
½ cup cocoa	¼ tsp. salt
1 tsp. soda	

Mix all ingredients until smooth. Drop by teaspoon onto cookie sheet. Bake for 10 minutes at 350°F. When cool, mix filling (below) and then sandwich together.

Filling

½ cup shortening	2 egg whites
1 tsp. vanilla	dash of salt
2 cups powdered sugar	

Homemade Tootsie Rolls

1 square unsweetened chocolate
¼ tsp. vanilla
1 ¼ cup (or more) powdered sugar
¼ cup + 2 tbsp. powdered milk

1 tbsp. butter
¼ cup dark Karo syrup

Melt chocolate and butter over low heat in a saucepan; remove from heat. Stir in syrup and vanilla and blend well. Add dry milk and 1 cup sifted powdered sugar. Stir well. Knead on wax paper until smooth, using sufficient powdered sugar to make pliable, easy-to-handle dough. Divide dough into tablespoon balls; roll into strips by hand. Cut into pieces and wrap in plastic and store in refrigerator.

Homemade Bits-O-Honey

½ cup honey
1 cup peanut butter

1 tbsp. butter
1 to 1 1/8 cups dry milk powder

Combine honey, butter, and peanut butter in bowl; mix well. Add enough dry milk to firm dough. Knead until smooth, shape into small rolls, and place on wax paper. Let stand until firm. Wrap each in wax paper. Makes 1 dozen.

Homemade Toffee

1 lb. butter
2 cups sugar
16 oz. milk chocolate chips

½ cup water
1 tsp. salt
candy thermometer

Bring butter, water, sugar, and salt to a boil over high heat in a saucepan. Stir constantly until temperature reaches 300°F, approximately 10 to 13 minutes. Pour into ungreased 10"× 13" pan and spread evenly to coat. Quickly sprinkle milk chocolate chips evenly over hot toffee and wait for

1 minute. Spread softened chocolate evenly over entire pan. Chill for 2 hours. Slam pan once on a counter to crack and break into 2 inch or smaller pieces. Store chilled in airtight plastic bag. Get to room temperature before serving.

Chocolate Truffles

36 oz. semisweet chocolate chips   2 tbsp. pure vanilla extract
28 oz. sweetened condensed milk   1 tbsp. coffee crystals, optional

Line a lot of cookie sheets with waxed paper. Combine the chips and milk in a heavy saucepan or large microwave bowl. Heat until melted smooth, stirring frequently. Do not overheat. Remove from heat; stir in vanilla and any additional flavored extract. Chill for 2 hours.

Form into 1-inch balls and place on prepared cookie sheets. Small ice cream scoop works well. Roll in powdered sugar or cocoa powder. Chill balls for 2 hours after formed if coating with melted chocolate, then dip in the chocolate with toothpicks and roll in desired coatings if desired. Roll immediately after balls are dipped in if using extra coatings. Let the balls sit for 3 hours. Store in a cool place in airtight container.

This recipe is a basic truffle recipe. Makes 12 dozen truffles. Cut the recipe in half if needed. Dip them into white chocolate and roll in red and green sugar or sprinkles for a festive look. One teaspoon of flavored extract can be added to a quarter of the dough for 4 different flavors or 4 teaspoons of flavor for the whole recipe.

Flavor variations are as follows: almond, orange, raspberry, cherry, rum, raspberry, peppermint, cinnamon oil, 1 tbsp. prepared coffee, flavored brandy, 2 tsp. balsamic vinegar

Coating variations are as follows: melted white chocolate, melted milk chocolate, melted bittersweet chocolate, powdered or granulated sugar, unsweetened cocoa, sprinkles/jimmies, red hots, finely chopped nuts, flaked coconut, crushed hard candies, nonpareils, crushed candy cane.

No-Bake Cookies

¼ cup butter

2 tbsp. cocoa

½ cup peanut butter

3 cups oatmeal

2 cups sugar

½ cup milk

1 tsp. vanilla

Over medium heat, bring butter, sugar, cocoa, and milk to a full boil. Boil for 1 minute. Add peanut butter and remove from heat when all is melted. Add vanilla and pour over oatmeal and mix well. Drop onto wax paper and let firm up. Ready in about 15 minutes. Makes 2 ½ dozen cookies.

Gingerbread Cookies

Dough

4 cups flour

2 tsp. cinnamon

½ tsp. nutmeg

½ tsp. baking soda

2/3 cup brown sugar

2/3 cup molasses

1 tbsp. ground ginger

1 tsp. salt

½ tsp. cloves

1 cup butter

2 large eggs

Icing

1 lb. powdered sugar

3 large egg whites

1 drop lemon juice

For the dough, sift the dry ingredients except sugar into a small bowl and whisk well to combine. Beat the butter and sugar and add 1 egg at a time, beating until smooth. Beat in ½ flour mixture; scrape down bowl often. Beat in molasses, scrape again, and beat in remaining flour mixture just until combined. Divide dough into several pieces, and press each piece into a rectangle about ¼ inch thick between 2 sheets of plastic wrap (this step is important). Chill the dough for 1 hour or until firm, can be overnight.

Set oven racks in the middle and two-thirds of oven. Preheat to 350°F. Roll dough, one piece at a time, on floured surface to make dough ¼-inch thick. Cut with floured cutters and arrange on pans about 1 inch apart. Reroll all extra dough; cut until all is gone. Bake for 8 to 10 minutes until firm. Remove from heat, cool a bit, then put on wire racks.

For the icing, combine the powdered sugar and egg whites in a bowl and beat well. Add lemon juice and beat until fluffy. Divide the icing into several bowls and add different food coloring to each for a variation. Spread icing over cookies. May decorate with raisins and sprinkles.

Rhubarb Coffee Cake

½ cup butter	1 ½ cups sugar
2 eggs	1 cup sour cream
1 tsp. vanilla	2 cups flour
1 tsp. baking soda	2 cups rhubarb, sliced

Topping

½ cup brown sugar, packed	1 tbsp. flour
1 tsp. cinnamon	1 tbsp. butter

Preheat oven to 350°F. Cream butter and sugar together; beat in eggs one at a time. Stir in sour cream and vanilla. Mix flour and baking soda and fold into batter. Stir in rhubarb. Turn into greased 9"× 13" pan. Mix topping ingredients together until crumbly. Sprinkle over top and bake for 30 to 40 minutes or until done.

Éclair Cake

1 lb. honey graham crackers

2 ¾ cups milk

2 small instant vanilla pudding

8 oz. Cool Whip

Frosting

1 pkg. Chocó-bake (unsweetened liquid chocolate)

2 tsp. white Karo syrup

2 tsp. vanilla

3 tbsp. butter, soft

1 ½ cups powdered sugar

3 tbsp. milk

Butter 9"× 13" pan and layer with whole graham crackers. Mix pudding and milk and blend in Cool Whip. Put ½ pudding mixture over crackers. Layer more crackers over pudding. Top with rest of pudding. Cover with a layer of crackers (third layer). Chill for 2 hours before frosting. Beat all frosting ingredients until smooth. Frost cake and chill for 2 hours. May be frozen.

Lemon Sauce for Bread Pudding

½ cup sugar

½ tsp. salt

2 tbsp. butter

3 ½ tbsp. lemon juice

1 ½ tbsp. cornstarch

1 cup

½ tbsp. lemon zest

3 drops lemon extract

In a saucepan, boil water. Combine sugar, starch, and salt; gradually add boiling water until smooth. Cook over low heat until thick and clear. Remove from heat, add rest of ingredients, and blend well. Serve warm.

Granny's Peanut Brittle

Mix together:
3 cups of sugar
1 cup water
1 cup white Karo syrup

Cook to 250°F. Add raw peanuts and stir. Bring to 325°F and remove from heat.

Stir in:
2 tbsp. butter
1 ½ tsp. vanilla
½ tsp. salt.

Add 1 tbsp. soda and pour into buttered pan. Do not spread.

Divinity

Cook 4 cups of sugar, 1 cup white Karo syrup, 1 cup hot water, and 1 tsp. salt. Cook until hard ball stage (288°F). Slowly pour over 2 egg whites beaten stiff. Beat and add 1 tsp. vanilla. Drop onto wax paper to harden.

Raisin Cream Pie

1 unbaked pie shell	2 eggs
1 cup sour cream	¾ cup sugar
¼ tsp. salt	¼ tsp. nutmeg
1 cup raisins	1 tsp. vanilla

Blend well, pour into pie shell, and bake at 375°F for 40 minutes or until set. Cool and serve.

Butter Crunch Bar

1 cup butter
1 cup sugar
1 egg
1 ½ cup flour
1 cup oatmeal
1 tsp. vanilla, orange, and coconut flavoring

Beat sugar and butter until creamy. Add egg, flavorings, and mix well. Add flour and oatmeal; mix well.

Spread in large cake pan. Top with colored sprinkles and bake 40 to 45 minutes at 275°F. Do not let get Brown. Cut while warm.

Or drop onto greased cookie sheet and bake for 35 minutes.

Granny's Favorite
Beverage Recipes

Homemade Soda Pop... page 199

Homemade
Lemon-Lime
Aide

Homemade Lemon-Lime Aide... page 198

Homemade Eggnog... page 202

Homemade Lemon-Lime Aide

1 ½ cups lemon juice (6 to 8 lemons)
¾ cup lime juice (8 to 10 limes)
8 cup water
1 cup sugar

Microwave lemons for 1 ½ minutes on high and limes for 1 minute for maximum juice. Combine juices in gallon container. Stir in sugar and water, chill and serve.

Homemade Lemonade

3 lemons, sliced   1 cup sugar water

Put lemons and sugar in 2-quart pitcher. With large spoon, pound lemons to release the juice, stir. Add a batch of ice cubes and let sit awhile. Add water to fill, mix, and serve.

Homemade Italian Ice

¾ cup frozen orange juice concentrate   2 cup ice cubes

Blend frozen juice concentrate and ice cube, 1 cube at a time, in blender until mix is smooth for about 2 minutes. Serve immediately or store in freezer. For variations, use other flavor concentrate such as apple, grape, or grapefruit for different tastes.

Homemade Blizzard

2 scoops vanilla ice cream   ½ cup milk   3 crushed cookies

Blend well and serve. For variations, use Oreos, chocolate chips, peanut butter, Heath bar, Butterfingers, Reese's pieces, or your favorite candy or cookie.

Homemade Soda Pop

6 oz. can frozen juice, apple, orange, grape, pineapple
seltzer or carbonated water, chilled

Stir 3 juice cans. Fill with seltzer or carbonated water in with frozen juice; mix well. Makes a great drink with less sugar than ordinary pop.

Homemade Root Beer

1 gal. warm water (110–115°F)
2 cups sugar
1 tsp. yeast
4 tsp. root beer extract

Mix all together well. Pour into small-necked 1-gallon glass jug, leaving no more than 1 ½ inches head space. Tightly cap. Allow to rest at room temperature for 3 hours. Chill and serve.

Homemade Ice Cream Sodas

Black and White Soda

¼ cup milk
chilled soda water
chocolate curls

3 tbsp. chocolate syrup
vanilla ice cream

In tall glass, pour milk, and add syrup and a scoop of ice cream. Fill with soda water. Garnish with chocolate curls.

For different variations, try the following:

Coffee Soda

3 tbsp. coffee syrup (see below)
vanilla ice cream
chocolate curls

¼ cup milk
chilled soda water

Coffee Syrup

In a saucepan, mix 1 cup sugar, 1 cup light corn syrup, and
1 ½ cups water and bring to a boil, stirring constantly. Remove from heat
and stir in ¼ cup instant coffee and 1 tsp. vanilla. Keep chilled.

Lemon Soda

¼ cup milk
vanilla ice cream

2 tbsp. frozen lemonade concentrate
chilled soda water

Fruity Soda

10 oz. sliced berries added to peaches, pureed
½ cup milk vanilla ice cream
chilled soda water

Homemade Cocoa Mix

2 lb. Nestle's Quick powder
8 qts. nonfat dry milk
8 oz. coffee creamer, powder
½ cup powdered sugar

Mix well, use ¼ cup mix in each mug. Fill with boiling water and stir. Store
in airtight container. May be garnished with marshmallows.

Homemade Tomato Juice Cocktail

1 ½ cup fresh tomatoes
2 bay leaves
3 tbsp. chopped onion
1 tbsp. worcestershire sauce
3 dashes Tabasco sauce

3 cup chopped celery
¾ cup chopped green pepper
1 ½ tsp. salt
1 ½ tsp. horseradish

In a pot, slowly cook tomatoes, celery, green pepper, bay leaf, and onion for 20 minutes. Process in blender; put through a sieve. Add salt, worcestershire sauce, Tabasco sauce, and horseradish; blend well. Chill for 3 hours. Serve with lemon wedges. Yields 8 to 9 cups.

Homemade Hot Buttered Rum Mix

2 lbs. brown sugar	1 ½ tsp. cinnamon
½ tsp. nutmeg	1 lb. butter, soft
1 tsp. vanilla	boiling water
1 bottle rum	

Mix brown sugar, cinnamon, nutmeg, and vanilla in soft butter. Freeze or refrigerate until ready to use. For each serving, add 1 tbsp. of mix to 6 oz. boiling water and 1 shot of rum. Great on a cold winter's night.

Homemade Eggnog

4 eggs, separated	1/3 cup + 1 tbsp. sugar
2 cups whole milk	1 cup heavy cream
1 tsp. nutmeg	1 tsp. vanilla

Separate eggs, set aside whites. Mix together egg yolks; add 1/3 cup sugar. Mix until dissolved; stir in milk, cream, nutmeg, and vanilla. Whip egg whites to soft peaks; add 1 tbsp. sugar. Beat until stiff peaks form. Whisk egg whites into mixture. Chill and serve.

Homemade Creme de Menthe

3 cups sugar	2 cups water
1 lemon, thinly sliced	1 1/3 cup vodka
½ tsp. peppermint extract	2 tsp. vanilla
green food coloring	

Combine sugar, water, and lemon in a saucepan. Bring to a boil, stirring constantly. Lower heat and simmer for 5 minutes. Strain. Cool. Stir in vodka, peppermint, vanilla, and a few drops food coloring, optional. Pour into an airtight container and allow to age for 1 week.

Homemade Kahlua

4 cups water

3 cups sugar

¾ cup instant coffee (not freeze-dried)

2 oz. vanilla extract or ¼ split vanilla beans

1/5 vodka

Simmer water and sugar. Remove from heat, and add coffee and vanilla. Cool, then add vodka. Let age for 4 weeks.

Homemade Irish Cream Liqueur

1 ¾ cup liqueur (Irish or rye whiskey, brandy, rum, bourbon, or scotch)

14 oz. sweetened condensed milk

1 cup heavy cream

4 eggs

2 tbsp. chocolate syrup

1 tsp. vanilla

½ tsp. almond extract

2 tsp. instant coffee

Combine ingredients in blender until smooth. Store in refrigerator up to one month. Stir before serving. Serve over ice.

Homemade Cream Liqueur

14 oz. sweetened condensed milk

1 cup heavy cream

4 eggs

1 ¼ cups favorite liqueur (amaretto, coffee, orange, or mint)

Combine all ingredients and blend until smooth. Serve over ice. Store tightly covered in refrigerator up to 1 month. Stir before using.

Homemade Amaretto

2 cups packed brown sugar	2 cups sugar 4 cups water
½ cup almond extract	½ gal. vodka

Combine brown sugar, sugar, and water in a saucepan. Bring to a rolling boil for 6 minutes, stirring constantly. Remove from heat and cool for about 4 hours at room temperature. Add almond extract and vodka. Bottle. Makes ¾ gallon.

Homemade Coffee liqueur

2 cups brown sugar	2 cups sugar
4 cups water	1 qt. vodka
2 oz. instant coffee	½ vanilla bean, split lengthwise

Dissolve sugars in water and bring to a boil. Remove from heat and add instant coffee. Cool completely. Add vanilla bean and vodka. Store in airtight jar for one month.

Homemade Orange Liqueur

1 cup sugar
½ cup water
3 cups brandy
2 tsp. orange extract

Dissolve sugar in almost boiling water. Place over low heat for 3 minutes, stirring constantly. Allow to cool. Add brandy and orange extract. Pour into airtight container. Stir or shake bottle each day to dissolve sugar completely. Let age for 10 days.

Sun Tea

1 gallon water
5 tea bags
lemon slices
ice

Fill gallon water to top and insert tea bags. Place in the sun for 2 hours at least until tea is desired strength; remove tea bags. Chill. Pour over ice in glass and garnish with lemon slices.

Granny's Favorite

Condiment Recipes

Homemade Steak Sauce... page 210

Homemade Sweet Tartar Sauce
also Dill Tartar Sauce...page 217

Homemade Butter... page 210

Homemade Sweetened Condensed
Milk... page 218

Chocolate Spread... page 220

Homemade Boursin Cheese...
page 222

Homemade Mayonnaise

¼ cup sugar	1 tsp. flour
1 tsp. dry mustard	½ tsp. salt
¼ cup water	¼ cup vinegar
2 eggs, beaten	1 tbsp. butter

Combine sugar, flour, dry mustard, and salt in a saucepan. Gradually stir in water, vinegar, beaten eggs, and butter and cook over medium heat to a boil, beating constantly. Cover and chill.

Quick Mayonnaise

1 cup olive oil	1 tsp. dijon mustard
1 egg	2 tbsp. vinegar or lemon

Blend mustard, vinegar, and egg. Beat well. Add oil a little at a time while beating. Chill.

Homemade Ketchup

1 gallon tomatoes
1 tbsp. mixed pickle spice
1 cup vinegar
¼ tsp. red pepper

1 large onion
1 cup sugar
2 tbsp. salt

Mix tomatoes, onion, and pickle spice in a saucepan and add ½ cup water to get started. Cook for about 1 hour, stirring occasionally until tender. Put in a cloth bag and drain for 1 hour. Cook tomato mix very slowly until thick. Add sugar, vinegar, salt, and red pepper. Boil this final mix for 10 minutes. Preserve by bottling and capping.

Homemade Mustard

1 cup dry mustard
2 eggs
pinch of salt

1 cup white vinegar
1 cup sugar

Mix together dry mustard and vinegar and let set overnight. The next day, add eggs, sugar, and salt. Cook on low heat until thick. Chill.

Homemade Hot Mustard

4 tsp. flour
½ tsp. dried mustard
vinegar to thin

2 tsp. sugar
pinch of turmeric

Mix ingredients. Chill for 2 hours. Serve over ham or other dishes where hot mustard is desired. (Turmeric is of the ginger family.)

Homemade Horseradish Mustard

2 vegetable bouillon cubes	1 ½ cup hot water
4 tsp. cornstarch	4 tsp. sugar
4 tsp. dry mustard	2 tsp. turmeric
¼ cup white vinegar	4 tsp. prepared horseradish
2 slightly beaten egg yolks	

Dissolve bouillon cubes in hot water. In a saucepan, blend cornstarch, sugar, mustard, turmeric, vinegar, and horseradish. Slowly blend in dissolved bouillon. Cook and stir over low heat until thick and bubbly. Gradually stir a moderate amount of thick mixture into the egg yolks. Return to saucepan; cook stirring constantly for about 1 minute. Cover and chill. Makes 1 ½ cups.

Homemade Honey

10 cups sugar
1 tsp. alum
66 clover blossoms

Combine sugar and alum with 2 ½ cups of warm water in a saucepan. Mix thoroughly and bring to a gentle boil for 10 minutes over medium heat without stirring. Remove from heat. Drop clover blossoms into hot liquid. Let stand for 10 minutes. Strain. Pour into sterilized jars. Yields 4 pints.

Homemade Gluten

5 lb. bread flour (high gluten)	5 cups cold water
½ tsp. salt	2 tbsp. Poultry Seasoning
1 tbsp. minced onion	

Mix flour and water to form stiff dough. Let stand covered with water for at least 15 minutes (up to overnight) in refrigerator. Knead under running water to wash starch out (until water is fairly clear). Work in salt, seasoning, and onion into gluten by hand. Cover with plastic wrap. Cook for 10 minutes in microwave, turn over, and repeat for other side. Cool. Use in recipes in place of burger. Freezing firms texture.

Homemade Egg Beaters

4 egg whites   1 tbsp. olive oil
1 tbsp. nonfat dried milk

Whip together until thoroughly blended. Use as would eggs.

Homemade Egg Beaters Cholesterol-Free

3 egg whites   3 tbsp. skim milk
1 tbsp. dry powdered milk   1 tsp. vegetable oil

Beat egg whites with fork; add remaining ingredients. Beat until thoroughly blended. Use as would eggs.

Homemade Whipping Cream

1 stick butter   ½ cup shortening
1 cup warm milk   2 tsp. vanilla

Mix butter, shortening, and vanilla, adding warm milk a little at a time while beating at high speed.

Homemade Sour Cream

For each quart of cream, add 2 tbsp. cider vinegar and 1 packet of Knox gelatin. Whip until it has the appearance of stiff whipped cream.

Homemade Butter

1 cup heavy cream
pinch of salt

Pour heavy cream into watertight container, cap. Shake vigorously for 30 to 40 minutes. Or put in butter churn and churn for 40 minutes. Pour off buttermilk; add a pinch of salt. Work the butter with a spoon; continue to pour off buttermilk as it comes out of butter. Refrigerate.

Homemade Peanut Butter

2 cups dry roasted peanuts
1 to 2 tbsp. peanut oil or vegetable oil
salt

Put 1 cup peanuts into the blender; blend at medium speed for 10 seconds. Scrape sides of blender. Add oil, cover, and blend mixture until smooth. Scrape peanut mixture into a mixing bowl. Repeat with remaining cup of peanuts. Combine both batches of peanut butter and taste. If necessary, add a little salt. Put peanut butter in jar and refrigerate until ready to use. Keep refrigerated.

Homemade Steak Sauce

1 cup ketchup	½ cup onion, coarsely chopped
¼ cup water	1 clove garlic, chopped finely
¼ cup worcestershire sauce	¼ cup lemon juice
¼ cup distilled white vinegar	2 tbsp. soy sauce
2 tbsp. brown sugar	1 tbsp. prepared mustard

Combine all ingredients in a saucepan. Simmer uncovered for 30 minutes or until it reaches a good consistency, stirring occasionally. Cool. Strain to remove onion and garlic. Store in refrigerator. Similar to A-1 sauce.

Homemade Sloppy Joe Sauce

1 cup chopped onion

1 cup chopped green pepper

1 tbsp. olive oil

1 tbsp. sugar

2 tbsp. prepared mustard

1 tsp. salt

1 cup ketchup

¼ tsp. powdered cloves

1 lb. lean ground beef

Brown lean ground beef in oil. Mix together all ingredients. Cover and simmer for 30 minutes.

Homemade Meat Sauce

green pepper

1 qt. crushed tomatoes

1 onion

mushrooms

Chop all and simmer over low heat for a few hours, and pour over favorite meat.

Homemade Italian Meat Sauce

1 cup chopped onion

2 cloves garlic, minced

¼ cup olive oil

1 lb. lean ground beef

2 Italian sausages, chopped

2 qts. sliced tomatoes

12 oz. tomato paste

2 tbsp. sugar

1 tbsp. leaf oregano

1 tbsp. leaf basil

1 tbsp. salt

½ tsp. pepper

¼ cup grated parmesan cheese

Sauté onion and garlic in olive oil until soft. Brown beef and sausage. Pour off all but 2 tbsp. fat in a skillet. Stir in tomatoes, tomato paste, sugar, crumbled oregano, crumpled basil, salt, and pepper. Simmer uncovered, stirring frequently, for 45 minutes or until sauce thickens. Stir in cheese, cool. Freeze in plastic container.

Homemade Marinara Sauce

5 tomatoes, chopped	30 oz. tomato sauce
1 can tomato paste	1 onion, chopped
3 cloves garlic, minced	1 bell pepper, diced
12 mushrooms, sliced	2 carrots, sliced
1 zucchini, sliced	1 tbsp. soy sauce
¼ cup red wine	2 bay leaves
1 tsp. black pepper	½ tbsp. basil
½ tbsp. oregano	¼ tsp. sage

Add all ingredients together, except dry herbs, and simmer for 2 hours. Add dry herbs and simmer for 2 hours longer.

Homemade Lasagna Sauce

16 oz. tomato sauce
16 oz. tomato paste
16 oz. tomatoes, whole
1 cup water
1 tbsp. each parsley, salt, pepper, onion salt, garlic salt
¼ tsp. baking soda
¼ tsp. sugar

Chop tomatoes and simmer with all ingredients for 30 minutes; stir often. Add 1 lb. lean ground beef, 2 lbs. ricotta cheese, and 2 eggs.

Homemade Teriyaki Marinade

½ cup soy sauce	¼ cup brown sugar
2 tbsp. lemon juice	1 tbsp. vegetable oil
¼ tsp. ginger	1/8 tsp. garlic

Mix ingredients. Allow chicken or beef to sit in marinade overnight. Refrigerate until ready to grill.

Homemade Thai Sauce for Fish

3 to 5 tbsp. oil

1 tsp. lemon juice

3 to 4 tbsp. cream peanut butter

3 to 4 tbsp. teriyaki

dash of pepper

Cover 9"× 13" pan with oil. Add teriyaki sauce and lemon juice. Mix in cream peanut butter. Lay seafood in mixture. Sprinkle seafood with black pepper. Spoon some of mixture on the top of seafood. Cover pan with plastic wrap; allow seafood to sit in marinade overnight. Refrigerate until ready to grill. Excellent with king or Spanish mackerel.

Easy Homemade BBQ Sauce

1 cup ketchup

2 tsp. chili powder

1 tsp. worcestershire sauce

1 cup water

1 tsp. mustard

¼ cup sugar

Combine all in a saucepan and bring to boil. Put in jar, let cool. Seal and refrigerate until ready to use.

Quick Homemade BBQ Sauce

2/3 cup ketchup

2 ½ tbsp. worcestershire sauce

4 tsp. brown sugar, packed

¼ tsp. each salt, crushed

4 tsp. olive oil

1 tsp. mustard

2 tbsp. red wine vinegar

dash of garlic

red pepper, black pepper

Whisk together all and brush on meat.

Chicken BBQ Sauce

1 cup chopped onion
8 tbsp. lemon juice
2 tsp. salt
2 tsp. paprika
1 tsp. curry powder

1 cup salad oil
1 cup brown sugar
4 tbsp. worcestershire sauce
4 cups tomato sauce

Sauté onions in oil. Add rest ingredients and simmer 30 minutes.

Finger Lickin' Good BBQ Sauce

½ white onion, chopped
3 tbsp. olive oil
1 2/3 cup ketchup
1/3 cup worcestershire sauce
cayenne pepper

3 cloves garlic, minced
½ cup white vinegar
1/3 cup brown sugar
2 tsp. chili powder

Cook onion and garlic until soft in olive oil. Add white vinegar, ketchup, brown sugar, worcestershire sauce, chili powder, and a dash of cayenne pepper. Simmer for 30 minutes.

Balsamic BBQ Sauce

1 tsp. olive oil
2/3 cups balsamic vinegar
1/3 cup brown sugar

2 tbsp. chopped onion
3 cups ketchup
1/3 cup honey

Sauté onions in olive oil over medium heat. Add balsamic vinegar and reduce heat by half. Add ketchup, brown sugar, and honey. Bring to a simmer and cook for 5 minutes, stirring constantly.

Homemade Tomato Sauce

1 clove garlic, minced	1 small onion, chopped
olive oil	28 oz. crushed tomatoes
6 oz. tomato paste	1 cup water
4 basil leaves or 2 tsp. dry basil	¼ tsp. black pepper
¾ tsp. salt	

Heat olive oil over medium heat. Brown garlic and sauté onions until transparent. Add crushed tomatoes, tomato paste blended with water, basil, pepper, and salt. Simmer for 30 minutes over low heat, stirring often.

Homemade Italian Tomato Sauce

½ cup olive oil
½ medium onion, chopped
8 cloves garlic, minced
12 oz. tomato paste
60 oz. tomato puree
1 tbsp. basil
2 tbsp. romano cheese, grated
½ tsp. salt
¼ tsp. sugar

Sauté onions and garlic in olive oil. Simmer until soft and golden. Add tomato paste and simmer until blended with oil for about 10 minutes. Add tomato puree and simmer for 15 minutes. Add sugar, salt, basil, cheese, and 6 oz. water. Simmer for 20 minutes, stirring constantly. With tilted lid, cover pot and simmer for 1 hour. Sauce will thicken.

Homemade Taco Sauce

1 lb. tomatoes

1 medium onion, chopped

1 cup ketchup

3 long hot green pepper, chopped or use hot sauce to taste

½ cup wine vinegar

2 bay leaves

1 tsp. Italian seasoning

1 tsp. garlic powder

2 tbsp. soy sauce

1 tsp. salt

1/3 cup sugar

1 tsp. lemon pepper

1 tsp. basil

Cook all ingredients together over low heat for 30 minutes, stirring occasionally. Makes about 3 cups of sauce.

Homemade Picante Sauce

28 oz. crushed tomatoes

1 medium onion chopped

1 tsp. white vinegar

½ to ¾ cup water

1 large jalapeño peppers or 5 slices

6 oz. tomato paste

1/8 tsp. garlic powder

1 tsp. salt

pinch of red cayenne pepper

Mix all in large bowl real well. Ready to eat. Refrigerate leftovers. Will keep for days. The longer the sauce sits, the hotter it gets.

Homemade Salsa

1 large can peeled tomatoes, drained and pureed

1 can stewed tomatoes	1 can chili tomato sauce
½ cup vinegar	1 can chili tomatoes
1 can tomato sauce	½ cup sugar
1 stalk celery, chopped	4 green peppers, chopped
4 yellow onions, chopped	3 bunches green onions red peppers

jalapeño peppers to taste (5 is mild)

Chop vegetables. Mix all ingredients. Cook over low heat until vegetables are tender. Refrigerate or jar for canning. Makes 4 quarts.

Homemade Sweet Tartar Sauce

1 egg	1 tbsp. minced garlic
2 tbsp. lemon juice	1 tbsp. chopped parsley
2 tbsp. chopped green onion	2 tbsp. drained sweet pickle relish
1 cup vegetable oil	¼ tsp. cayenne pepper
1 tbsp. mustard	1 tsp. salt

Put egg, garlic, lemon juice, parsley, green onion, and relish in blender for 15 seconds. With motor running, pour in oil in steady stream. Stop motor. Add cayenne, mustard, salt, and pulse to blend. Cover and let sit for 1 hour in refrigerator before using. Use within 24 hours.

Homemade Dill Tartar Sauce

2 cups mayonnaise	¼ onion, diced
1 dill pickle, chopped	1 tsp. worcestershire sauce
1/3 tsp. cream of tartar	1 ½ tsp. lemon juice
2 drops Tabasco sauce	

Beat all ingredients together for 1 minute to make it fluffy. Serve.

Homemade Sweetened Condensed Milk

1 cup sugar   ½ cup water
1/3 cup butter   1/3 cup dry milk

In a saucepan, combine sugar, water, and butter. Bring to boil, stirring constantly. Cool slightly. Put in blender and add dry milk. Blend until smooth. Makes 14 oz. equal to 1 can.

Homemade Maple Syrup

4 cups sugar   ½ cup brown sugar, packed
2 cups water   1 tsp. vanilla
1 tsp. maple flavor

Mix sugars and water in a saucepan; bring to boil, stirring until sugars dissolve. Reduce heat and cover. Boil gently for 10 minutes. Remove from heat and add both flavorings. Stir until mixed. Makes 1 quart.

Homemade Molasses

3 gal. green tomatoes
6 lbs. white sugar

Slice 2 gallons of green tomatoes. Each gallon should be heaped up. A gallon crock is good to measure with. Use 2 lbs. of sugar for each pound of tomatoes. Let set for 4 hours until juice raises some. Then put on stove and cook well. Take off stove and drain and strain through a colander to get the seeds out of the juice. Boil this juice down to the likeness of heavy syrup. Put in small jars for storage.

Blueberry Syrup

1 pint blueberries, rinsed, stems removed

1 cup sugar

¼ cup water

In a saucepan, cook all over medium heat, stirring until sugar dissolves. Crush berries slightly until mixture gets syrupy for about 10 to 12 minutes. Serve warm or cool.

Cheese Fondue

½ lb. swiss cheese, shredded

2 tbsp. cornstarch

1 cup white wine, dry

1 tbsp. cherry brandy

pinch of nutmeg

½ lb. gruyere cheese, shredded

1 clove garlic, peeled

1 tbsp. lemon juice

½ tsp. dry mustard

In a bowl, coat all cheese with cornstarch and set aside. Rub the inside of a fondue pot with garlic and discard. Over medium heat, add the wine, lemon juice, and simmer gently. Gradually stir in cheese. Melt cheese gradually for smooth fondue. When smooth, stir in cherry brandy, mustard, and nutmeg. Serve with pumpernickel bread, Granny Smith apples, broccoli, cauliflower, carrots, or asparagus. (Gruyere cheese is a yellow swiss cheese heavy in butterfat.)

Clotted Cream

2 cups pasteurized cream

Set a coffee filter basket lined with filter in a strainer over a bowl. Pour the cream almost to the top of filter. Refrigerate for 2 hours. The whey will sink to the bottom, passing through the filter, leaving a ring of clotted cream.

Scrape this down with a rubber spatula and repeat every couple of hours until the mass reaches the consistency of soft cream cheese.

Chocolate Spread

7 oz. dark chocolate
½ cup cream
¼ cup ground hazelnuts

Place chocolate and cream in a saucepan over low heat and simmer. Stir until chocolate melts; remove from heat, and stir in hazelnuts. Leave to cool until smooth enough to spread. Great over toast, pancakes, or cookies.

Homemade Ricotta Cheese

½ gal. whole milk   1 cup heavy cream
1 tsp. salt   2 ½ tbsp. white vinegar or 2 tbsp. lemon juice

Place milk, cream, and salt in large saucepan. Cook on medium-high heat until mixture comes to a full boil. Immediately remove from heat; add the vinegar. Stir. Let cool. Strain through cheesecloth-lined colander over a bowl. Makes about 1 ½ lbs. of ricotta cheese.

Homemade Cream Cheese

1 qt. buttermilk
1 qt. boiling water

Mix well and let stand for 20 minutes. Strain through double cheesecloth. Do NOT squeeze, just let drip. Hang in well-ventilated area for 2 to 3 sunny days. If weather is damp, will take longer. Do NOT hang in direct sunlight. Keep in tight container in refrigerator.

Homemade Cottage Cheese

1 2/3 cups instant nonfat dry milk
3 ¾ cups water
½ cup buttermilk

Mix and stir until smooth. Allow to clabber at room temperature overnight. Refrigerate until well chilled. Pour in cloth-lined colander placed over a pan and let all the whey drain. Season to taste. Refrigerate leftovers.

Homemade Cheese Spread

2 lbs. cottage cheese	1 tsp. baking soda
1 stick butter salt	½ cup heavy cream
1/3 cup dry grated parmesan cheese	caraway seeds (optional)
yellow food coloring (optional)	

Drain cottage cheese in strainer overnight. Place drained curds in a bowl, and stir in baking soda. Set aside at least 3 hours. The curds will bubble and become almost translucent. In a large saucepan, melt butter over low heat. Add curd and continue to stir. When partially melted, add ½ cup cream, dry grated parmesan cheese, and salt to taste. Cook slowly until melted. Pour in bowl to cool. May add caraway and food coloring. Delicious spread on fresh-baked bread.

Homemade Cheese

8 oz. diced Swiss cheese	1 ½ cups milk
¾ stick butter	1 ½ tsp. flour
caraway seeds	

In a heavy pot, put cheese, butter, 1 cup milk. Mix flour with ½ cup milk, like gravy, in a pot and add to other ingredients. Bring to boil, then cool and pour into airtight container. This will thicken as it cools. Store in refrigerator. Good for weeks.

Homemade Cheez Whiz

1 lb. American cheese, grated   1 tsp. dry mustard
12 oz. can evaporated milk   4 tbsp. butter

Melt over low heat until smooth the cheese, mustard, and milk. Beat in butter. Makes 1 quart. Very good.

Homemade Boursin Cheese

¼ tsp. each basil, dill weed, marjoram, thyme, and black pepper

In a large bowl or food processor, beat cheese and butter until fluffy. Add remaining ingredients and beat until well blended. Pack cheese into containers and cover tightly. Let mellow at least 12 hours. Will keep 2 to 4 weeks or can be frozen.

Homemade Devonshire Cream

8 oz. cream cheese, soft
½ cup sour cream
2 tbsp. powdered sugar

In a bowl, beat cream cheese until fluffy. Beat in sour cream and sugar until well mixed. Spoon into bowl and refrigerate until ready to serve. Makes 1 1/3 cups. To use, serve over fruit or cookies.

Homemade Vanilla Extract

1 cup brandy
2 vanilla beans, cut into 1-inch pieces

Combine brandy and vanilla beans in a ½ pint jar with a tight lid. Cover and let stand for 3 months, shaking 3 times a week. Yields 1 cup.

OR

2 cups vodka
5 vanilla beans, cut into 1-inch pieces

Combine vodka and vanilla beans in pint jar with tight lid. Cover and let stand for 6 to 8 weeks. Vodka mixture will turn amber colored in a day or two. After half the vanilla extract is used, add more vodka to cover the beans. The flavor in the beans is gone when vodka no longer turns a darker color.

OR

1 vanilla bean, coarsely chopped
1 cup dark rum

Put vanilla bean in a ½ pint jar and cover with rum. Cap the jar, cover, and let stand for 6 weeks. Shake the jar once a week. Strain the vanilla extract through a cheesecloth-lined strainer and into a sealed ½ pint jar.

OR

Place 3 to 4 vanilla beans in a ½ pint jar and fill with ½ vodka and ½ rum (or just vodka alone will do). In three weeks, extract is ready to use. You can leave the beans in the vodka; they will eventually dissolve over time. Or you can remove the vanilla beans and then store them in a jar filled with sugar for 3 months. This is vanilla sugar; you can use it in pies and cookies, sprinkle on desserts or in whipped cream, etc. Shake up the jar to blend well before using.

Try one or all of these variations. They are all equally wonderful.

Homemade Mint Extract

1 lb. of fresh spearmint or peppermint leaves
qt. vodka

Harvest mint leaves at noontime on a sunny day. Wash and crush/bruise the leaves. Add them to 1 quart of vodka and place in the sun for 3 or 4 weeks. Strain through cheesecloth and discard used leaves.

Citrus Extracts

orange zest or lemon peel
fruit pulp
vodka

Remove peel with zesting tool; do not get any white pith, which is bitter. Squeeze the fruit then strain the seeds and membranes; place peels and fruit pulp into a quart jar, filling 1/3 of the jar. Add vodka to fill. Use tight lid, cover, and let set for 6 weeks.

Anise Extract

Fill a ½ pint jar with whole star anise. Fill with vodka; leave indefinitely. Star anise also stores well in sugar to make anise-flavored sugar. Star anise are the star-shaped seed pods from the fruit of a Chinese evergreen tree that provides a key ingredient used in the production of Tamiflu, an antiviral agent purportedly effective in fighting the flu.

Homemade Coffee Extract

¼ lb. coffee
1 ½ qt. cold water

Add coffee to a 2-quart container and add water and mix well. Cap and refrigerate for 48 hours. Put coffee through a paper cone strainer or cheesecloth. Keep refrigerated until ready to use. Dilute with hot or cold water for beverage.

Homemade Cake Flour

2 cups minus 2 tbsp. flour
2 tsp. baking powder
2 tbsp. cornstarch

Stir all together; mix well. This turns all-purpose flour into cake flour.

Homemade Baking Powder

2 tbsp. cream of tartar
1 tbsp. baking soda
1 tbsp. cornstarch

Sift all together. Store in airtight container. One teaspoon of homemade baking powder is equal to one teaspoon of Royal baking powder.

Homemade Brown Sugar

2 to 3 cups sugar
¼ cup molasses

Mix together for brown sugar.

Homemade Curry Powder

4 ½ tsp. ground coriander

1 ¼ tsp. cumin seed

1 tsp. crushed red pepper

½ inch stick cinnamon

¼ tsp. ground ginger

2 tsp. ground turmeric

1 tsp. whole black peppercorns

½ tsp. whole cardamom seed
(without pods)

¼ tsp. whole cloves

In blender, place all spices and blend for 2 minutes or until mixture is a fine powder. Store spice mixture in an airtight container in a cool, dry place. Makes about ¼ cup curry powder.

Homemade Allspice

ground cinnamon
ground cloves
ground nutmeg

Mix equal parts of each spice to get allspice.

Homemade Pumpkin Pie Spice

¼ cup ground cinnamon

1 tbsp. nutmeg

1/8 cup ground ginger

1 tbsp. ground cloves

Mix all together. Store in airtight container; shake before using.

Homemade Sweet Spice Blend

1 tbsp. finely grated orange or lemon peel
2 tbsp. ground cinnamon
1 tbsp. each ground nutmeg, cloves, and ginger

Spread orange peel on waxed paper; let stand uncovered for 10 minutes. Mix peel thoroughly with spices. Store in an airtight container. Makes 1/3 cup. Add 2 or 3 tbsp. of this mix to cake or quick bread batter, ice cream, yogurt, or fruit.

Homemade Salt Substitute

1 tbsp. dry mustard   1 tbsp. onion powder

1 tbsp. paprika   1 tsp. garlic powder

½ tsp. white pepper   ¼ tsp. ground basil

Mix thoroughly. Store in salt shaker and use in place of salt.

Homemade Taco Seasoning Mix

1 tbsp. chili powder

2 tsp. onion powder

½ tsp. salt

1 tsp. each cumin, garlic powder, paprika, powdered oregano, and sugar

Mix all together well. Makes 3 tbsp. of seasoning mix, equal in strength to ¼ oz. pkg. commercial mix.

Homemade Spaghetti Sauce Mix

1 tbsp. each instant minced onion, parsley flakes, cornstarch

2 tsp. green pepper flakes

1 ½ tsp. salt

½ tsp. instant minced garlic

1 tsp. sugar

¾ tsp. Italian seasoning.

Mix all well. Makes 1 package of mix.

Homemade Onion Salt

Slice 2 white onions. In single layers, rings separated, place on cookie sheet. Oven dry at 200°F for 1 hour or until quite crisp, but not overly brown. Cool and place in blender. Whirl to a powder, using pulse. Add to onion ½ cup iodized salt and 1 tbsp. cornstarch. Blend 3 minutes longer. Place in tight container at room temperature 1 week before using.

Homemade Meat Seasoning

2 ¼ oz. can paprika	1 2/3 oz. celery salt
3 ¼ oz. onion salt	3 ¼ oz. garlic salt
1 tbsp. poultry seasoning	1 tbsp. salt

Mix all well. Put in seasoning jar with sprinkle lid. May be used on all meat and poultry.

Homemade Shake-and-Bake Mix

½ cup cornmeal	½ cup sifted flour
1 ½ tsp. salt	½ tsp. onion salt
½ tsp. pepper	½ tsp. ground oregano
2 tsp. chili powder	¼ tsp. garlic powder

Mix all well and coat your chicken or pork chops and bake as usual.

Crab Boil Spices

¼ cup pickling spices	¼ cup sea salt
2 tbsp. mustard seeds	2 tbsp. whole black peppercorns
2 tbsp. red pepper flakes	1 tbsp. celery seeds
1 tbsp. dried chives, minced	2 tsp. ginger
2 tsp. oregano	5 bay leaves

Put all in blender and pulse to a powder. For cooking shrimp, add ¼ cup of this spice along with 2 tsp. salt to large pan of boiling water or ½ boiling water and ½ beer.

Baharat a.k.a. Middle East Mixed Spices

1/2 cup whole black peppercorns
¼ cup whole coriander seeds
¼ cup cassia or cinnamon bark
¼ cup whole cloves
1/3 cup cumin seeds
2 tsp. whole cardamom seeds
4 whole nutmegs (or ¼ cup ground nutmeg)
½ cup ground paprika

Blend all but paprika and nutmeg in a blender to powder. Grate nutmeg and blend this with the paprika into the spices. Store in airtight container. This is a month's supply for a family living in Jordan.

Southwest Seasoning

2 tbsp. chili powder
1 tbsp. paprika
1 tbsp. ground coriander
2 tsp. cayenne pepper
1 tbsp. garlic powder

2 tsp. ground cumin
1 tsp. black pepper
1 tbsp. salt
1 tbsp. dried oregano
1 tsp. red pepper, crushed

Blend all well.

Homemade Waffle, Shortcake, Biscuit Mix

2 cups shortening   9 cups sifted flour   1 tbsp. salt   ¼ cup baking powder

Sift together dry ingredients. Add shortening. By hand, mix until crumbly. Ready to use. Store in closed container in pantry.

Crisp Waffles

1 ½ cup mix   2 tbsp. sugar   1 egg, separated   1 cup milk

Blend mix and sugar. Gradually add beaten egg yolk mixed with milk. Mix thoroughly. Fold in stiffly beaten egg white. Pour about ½ of mixtures in heated waffle iron and bake.

Shortcake

3 cups mix   3 tbsp. sugar   1 egg, beaten   ½ cup milk

Blend mix and sugar, add egg and milk, and stir with fork until all is moist. Turn dough onto waxed paper and knead 6 times. Place in 8-inch baking dish. Bake at 425°F for 15 minutes. Cool.

Biscuits

2 cups mix   ½ cup milk

Combine mix and milk to make dough. Turn out onto waxed paper and knead 6 times. Cut into biscuits and bake at 425°F for 15 minutes or until golden brown.

Homemade Cereal No. 1

6 cups oatmeal   3 cups coconut
1 cup wheat germ   1 cup honey
1 cup sunflower seeds   ½ cup oil
1 cup water   1 cup almonds

Mix oatmeal, coconut, wheat germ, and sunflower seeds in large bowl. Add honey, oil, water, and mix well. Bake on cookie sheet at 225°F for 2 ½ hours. Add almonds (may substitute walnuts) during last ½ hour. Stir mix on cookie sheet every 15 minutes. After cooling, put cereal in airtight container. Ready to eat, serve with milk.

Homemade Cereal No. 2

8 cups oatmeal	½ cup oil
½ cup honey	1 cup coconut
2 cups sliced almonds	2 cups raisins
1 cup chopped dates	¾ cup toasted wheat germ

Preheat oven to 350°F. In 9"× 13" buttered baking pan, put oatmeal and bake for 10 minutes. Stir in mixture of honey, oil, coconut, and almonds. Bake for 45 minutes, stirring every 10 minutes until brown; watch carefully. Cool; add raisins, dates, and toasted wheat germ. Ready to eat. Serve with milk.

Homemade Cereal No. 3

5 cups oatmeal plus 1 cup of each of the following: sliced almonds, sesame seeds, sunflower seeds, shredded coconut, soy flour, powdered milk, wheat germ, honey, vegetable oil

In a large bowl, combine all dry ingredients. In a small bowl, mix honey and oil. Combine all together. Spread on 2 cookies sheets. Bake at 300°F for 20 minutes. Stir and bake for 20 more minutes until slightly brown. Serve with milk.

Soup / Stew Recipes

Granny's Hamburger Soup – page 235

Tomato Soup – page 236

Cream of Potato Soup – page 233

Chicken Noodle Soup – page 232

Chicken Noodle Soup

4 to 5 lb. roasting chicken	1 large onion, chopped
2 tsp. salt	4 stalks celery, chopped
4 carrots, chopped	1 tsp. dill
1 tsp. parsley	¼ tsp. sage
egg noodles	

Place chicken pieces in large soup pot with water. Bring to boil for 15 minutes. Remove meat, cool a bit, debone, and skin. Cool soup, and skim off fat. Return meat to broth, add veggies and seasonings, and simmer for 2 hours. Add noodles, cook for 20 minutes, and serve.

Cream of Potato Soup

Cube a pot of potatoes. Add water, butter, and salt. Stew potatoes until tender. When done, mix 1 glass of cream with 1 tbsp. flour. Mix well; add to potatoes. Boil rapidly for 3 minutes. Remove from heat. Soup will thicken as it cools. Add white pepper. Fry bacon; crumble into soup.

Cream of Broccoli Soup

4 potatoes, peeled and cubed
16 oz. cut broccoli
13 oz. chicken broth
1 ½ cups shredded medium cheddar cheese
13 oz. evaporated milk
1 tbsp. dried onion flakes
thickening (about ½ cup flour to 1 cup water in shaker)

Cook potatoes in salted water until tender. Add broccoli and cook; drain. Add chicken broth, milk, onions, and cheese. Bring to boil, stirring constantly. Add thickening until creamy. Remove from heat and serve.

Cream Soup Mix

2 cups dry milk	¾ cup cornstarch
¼ cup dried onion flakes	1 tsp. basil
1 tsp. thyme	½ tsp. pepper

Combine all ingredients and mix well. Store in airtight container until ready to use.

Equal to 1 can of creamy condensed soup. Combine 1/3 cup soup mix and 1 ¼ cups cold water in a saucepan. Cook over medium heat, stirring until thickened.

For variations, add chopped mushrooms, celery, chicken.

Cheese Soup

1 small head cabbage, grated
1 cup carrots, grated
1 small onion, chopped
1 cup celery, chopped
9 cups water
1 can cream of chicken soup or 1/3 dry soup mix and 1 ¼ cup cold water
1 cup butter
1 cup flour
2 cups milk
2 lbs. Velveeta
¼ tsp. pepper
1 can stewed tomatoes

Boil carrots, cabbage, celery, onion, soup, and water until veggies are tender. Set aside.

For sauce: In a skillet, add butter, flour, and milk. Bring to boil and simmer for 20 minutes. Add to veggie mixture and cook until smooth. Add cheese, pepper, and drained tomatoes. Cook until cheese is all melted. Serve hot.

Creamy Ham Soup

3 cups potatoes, peeled and cubed
1 tsp. salt
1 garlic clove, chopped
3 tbsp. flour

2 cups water
¾ cup onion, chopped fine
4 tbsp. butter
4 cups milk

12 oz. Velveeta cheese, grated

2 cups ham, cooked and cubed

¼ tsp. black pepper

1/8 tsp. red pepper

1 tbsp. chopped fresh parsley

1 cup cooked broccoli

1 cup cooked cauliflower

Bring water, salt, and potatoes to boil. Cook until tender. In a dutch oven, cook onion and garlic in butter for 3 minutes. Drain potatoes and set aside. Gradually add flour to onions and stir well. Pour milk in 1 cup at a time. Cook over medium heat until hot. Simmer and add remaining ingredients. Stir until cheese is melted; simmer for 20 minutes. Serve.

Granny's Hamburger Soup

1 small onion, chopped

Garlic

olive oil

1 lb. lean ground beef

salt and pepper

8 cups water

1 cup celery, chopped

1 cup diced carrots

2 beef bouillon cubes

1 lb. potatoes, cubed

1 qt. stewed tomatoes

¼ cup flour

1 cup cream or milk

Cook onion in garlic olive oil until tender, and brown meat spiced with salt and pepper. Put in soup pot; add water, veggies, bouillon; and bring to boil. Simmer for 2 hours. Add flour and cream mix to thicken. Cook for 20 minutes and serve. This is Grandpa's favorite.

Bean Soup

1 lb. beans of choice
1 cup ketchup
1 tbsp. mustard
stewed tomatoes
1 cup celery, chopped
1 ham bone
2 cups ham, chopped
salt and pepper
1 large onion, chopped

Soak beans overnight in bowl with water 2 inches above beans. Cover with towel. Next day, rinse beans. Cover beans in pot with water. Bring to boil for several minutes. Reduce heat to simmer, and add remaining ingredients. Simmer for 3 hours. Serve

Tomato Soup

3 cups milk
1 pint cream
4 cans whole tomatoes
½ cup butter
dash of baking soda
salt and pepper
celery and onion powder

Cook milk and cream on low in soup pot; simmer. In another pot, cook tomatoes until boil, add baking soda, continue to boil, and skim off foam. Add tomatoes to milk; mix a little at a time so milk does not curdle. Stir in butter, season, and serve.

Granny's Beef Stew

Stew meat
1 can of each: carrots, corn, peas, green beans, tomatoes
1 cup celery, chopped
1 cup onion, chopped
1 can tomato paste
2 large potatoes, peeled and cubed
4 bay leaves
garlic
salt and pepper

Brown stew meat in olive oil. Put in soup pot; add veggies and spices. Bring to boil for several minutes. Turn to simmer for rest of the day, stirring frequently. Stew will thicken. Serve hot with biscuits or corn bread.

Quick Stew

stew meat, sliced thinly
1 large potato, diced
1 tbsp. A-1 sauce

can peas and carrots
1 tbsp. worcestershire sauce

Brown stew meat, put in pot with potatoes, water, and salt. Boil for 5 minutes, simmer, and add peas, carrots, sauces. Cook for 20 minutes. Serve.

I hope you have enjoyed reading
and cooking with

Granny's Favorites Cookbook

I really had a wonderful time putting this book together. It brought back
great memories of my childhood, when I first fell in love with cooking.
I will always remember my mother and
my granny's humming a tune in the kitchen
while cooking up one of their amazing meals.
They taught me that cooking is a joy,
and the wonderful aromas that
fill your home are priceless.

Please let me know if you have any questions.
I would love to hear about your cooking adventures.

Contact me at *TheDeedolCollection@nwi.net*

Dee Schoenmakers, Author of
Granny's Favorites Cookbook
Granny's Favorite Canning and Preserving Cookbook
Deedolicious! Granny's Favorite Cookie Recipes

Made in the USA
Las Vegas, NV
30 August 2021

29284492R00163